Ready-to-Use

PRE-SPORT
SKILLS
ACTIVITIES
PROGRAM

L.F. "BUD" TURNER ♦ SUSAN L. TURNER

**THE CENTER FOR APPLIED
RESEARCH IN EDUCATION**
West Nyack, New York 10994

Library of Congress Cataloging-in-Publication Data

Turner, Lowell F.
  Ready-to-use pre-sport skills activities program : 100 month-by-month
lessons with activities, games & assessments for the elementary
grades / Bud and Sue Turner.
        p.   cm.
  ISBN 0-13-026252-8
  1. Physical education for children—Study and teaching
(Elementary)—Activity programs—United States.   I. Turner, Susan
Lilliman,   II. Title.
GV223.T87   2000
372.86—dc21

                                          99-42151
                                          CIP

© 2000 *by* Parker Publishing Company, West Nyack, NY

Acquisitions Editor: *Connie Kallback*
Production Editor: *Mariann Hutlak*
Formatting: *TSI Graphics*

Printed in the United States of America

10 9 8 7 6 5 4 3 2 1

ISBN 0-13-026252-8

PARKER PUBLISHING COMPANY
West Nyack, New York 10994
www.phedu.com

Foreword

In recent years, a new national trend has emerged that takes a more serious look at the connection between physical activity and associated long-term health risks. Based on state and national health data, the national Centers for Disease Control and Prevention (CDC) has formally established the importance of schools to provide a well-rounded elementary physical education program.

At the same time, we have seen a growing body of scientific evidence from neuroscientists and child development experts that support the linkage between a child's attainment of basic motor skills and the development of the brain. This new research supports the notion that a child's natural inclination for physical activity plays an important role in the basic maturation of the brain and, therefore, the child's intellect. *In other words, there is a positive relationship between being physically fit and academically fit.*

As we enter the 21st century, elementary physical education teachers, classroom teachers, and parents must be able to respond to meeting the important fitness and motor development needs of young children. It is for this reason that I am excited to write this foreword for Bud and Sue Turner's latest publication, **Ready-to-Use Pre-Sport Skills Activities Program.** This new resource is a complete physical education curriculum guide for grades K–6. It offers an outstanding and practical approach for enhancing the fitness and motor development skills of young children in a clear and understandable fashion.

As a former elementary physical education teacher, I am pleased to see the wide variety of ready-to-use lessons and activities, cooperative activities, take-home activity sheets, monthly fitness calendars, and other innovative teaching ideas. Using a month-by-month overview, **Ready-to-Use Pre-Sport Skills Activities Program** provides an ideal way to develop a comprehensive physical education program for K–6 students.

Artie Kamiya, Section Chief for Healthful Living Education
North Carolina Department of Public Instruction
Great Activities Publishing Co., Editor
Raleigh, North Carolina

Acknowledgments

The authors wish to thank the talented individuals assisting with this project: Don Zemke for his photographic excellence and Ann Fujii Lindwall for her creative packaging of this text.

Dedication

This book is dedicated to those individuals understanding the importance of early planned, purposeful, physical education programs for children in preschool and the elementary grades.

About the Authors

Bud Turner, M.Ed., has been the Coordinator for K–12 Physical Education for Seattle Public Schools since 1979. He is an adjunct faculty member for Western Washington University, the University of Washington, and Seattle Pacific University. Mr. Turner has authored six other physical education texts and is in constant demand as a speaker on success-oriented physical education. Bud has worked as an advisor for P.E. TV, is an editorial board member for TEPE magazine, is a member of the NASPE Promotion Committee, and is an Advisory Board Member for U.S. Games. He is the recipient of AAHPERD's City and County Directors National Honor Award, Western Washington University's Professional Excellence State Award, American Cancer Society Volunteer Award, United States Tennis Association Honor Award, and the USA Today's Excellence Award.

Sue Turner, M.A., is a State Demonstration Teacher for the Seattle Public Schools. The co-author of six physical education texts, Sue has been honored for her excellence by being named Washington Elementary Physical Education Teacher of the Year, Seattle Schools' "Top Ten Teacher," and is the recipient of the Acorn Award presented by the Seattle Council PTSA. In 1998 *The Seattle Times Pacific Magazine* recognized her as one of Seattle's 20 most influential people in the area of fitness. In 1991 her students won the State Fitness Championship. Since 1972, Sue has directed the well-known SCATS (Seattle Public Schools Physical Education Demo Team). This talented group has completed over 400 goodwill performances including three AAHPERD national conventions. With 29 years of experience, Sue is a regular presenter around the Northwest. Together with her husband, Bud, they have presented more than 500 workshops on the "new" physical education.

About This Resource

It could be called reverse age discrimination as scores of American elementary students are denied the opportunity to increase their kinesthetic potential simply because they are considered to be too young. When faced with budget cuts, school districts have historically favored maintaining secondary programs with the assumption that younger students do not need or are not physically or emotionally ready for these experiences.

In reality, such developmental delays put these children further and further behind. Skills don't suddenly appear in junior high. They are developed, and the best place to acquire these **pre-sport** skills is the same place where math, reading, and language skills are learned—in the elementary grades.

Ready-to-Use Pre-Sport Skills Activities Program offers a library of 100 easy-to-use theme-oriented lesson plans featuring a four-step movement lesson format that ensures developmentally appropriate opportunities for individual and group interactions, cooperation, and, most important, variety. Weekly lesson plans are supplemented with daily take-home challenges, similarly designed monthly fitness calendars including July and August for optional use, 43 educational games, sample assessment tools, motivational reproducibles, and National Physical Education Standards for the elementary grades.

How The Lessons Work

Units

Each unit includes ten theme-oriented lesson plans. Every lesson is accompanied by a separate take-home assignment. These experiences are intended to be shared with other family members.

Lessons

The lesson format features four different but related parts. All of the components relate to the theme at hand. Each task is scripted, allowing immediate implementation by you.

- Warm-up: Each lesson offers a different warm-up. Warm-ups have a duration of no more than three to four minutes.

- Concept: The concept activities reinforce the theme by painting a kinesthetic picture for the students.

- Challenge: This component is often the students' favorite. Challenge activities invoke a friendly competition between partners without fear of being eliminated.

- Closer: This is meant to provide an active and successful end to the day's lesson.

Take-Home Activities

Typically, elementary-aged students spend about six hours in school and another five or six at home prior to going to sleep.

Research has shown that planned, purposeful movement experiences are essential to the growth, health, and happiness of children. While more districts across the country are providing instructional minutes outside of regular recesses, it is not enough.

For children to obtain and maintain a productive level of physical and health-related fitness, it's not only what we can motivate them to do at school, but at home as well.

If we can access just a few minutes of this out-of-school time by providing relevant and challenging pre-game skills, the possibilities for skill enhancement are endless.

Calendar Calisthenics

Calendar Calisthenics is a voluntary daily fitness supplement conducted outside of school. Monthly calendars accompany each theme-oriented set of ten lessons. Students take the calendars home, post them on refrigerators, and check off daily the tasks as they are completed. Parent participation is encouraged both as a checker and exercise partner. The small signature box in each corner allows parents to certify completion. Most programs implementing this motivational device have an incentive plan for students returning their calendars at the end of the month.

Small doses of creative exercises can move children toward more consistent patterns. Children will also find some mind and muscle activities to provide links between the classroom and the gymnasium.

Pre-Sport Skills for Elementary Children—<u>LESSON THEMES</u>

SEPTEMBER
<u>Working Together</u>
- Threesomes
- Opposing Forces
- Helping Hands
- One Step Back
- Cooperative Strength Training
- One-on-One
- Cooperative Challenges
- With Hands Held
- Friends Together
- Teamwork

CALENDAR

OCTOBER
<u>Speed</u>
- Reflex
- Quick Feet
- Accelerate
- Charge
- On Your Mark, Get Set, Go
- Slo Mo
- Jump City
- Pace
- Get a Clue
- Pursuit

CALENDAR

NOVEMBER
<u>Offense and Defense</u>
- Quick as a Cat
- Hands Up
- Pass It
- Take-Aways
- Beat the Clock
- Dodge City
- Foot Power
- Volleying
- Shielding
- Guarding

CALENDAR

DECEMBER
<u>Mind and Muscle</u>
- Colors
- Traffic Control
- Movement Math
- Notorious Bones
- Measurements
- Letters
- In Order
- Modes of Transportation
- Science
- Odd and Even

CALENDAR

JANUARY
<u>Heart Healthy</u>
- Aerobic
- Pump It Up
- Things You Can Control
- Minute Masters
- Keep It Up
- At Risk
- Relays
- Nutrition/Exercise
- Stress Reduction
- Home Fit

CALENDAR

FEBRUARY
<u>Sending and Receiving</u>
- Side to Target
- On the Move
- Implements
- Hit the Target
- Cross Dominance
- Right Back at Ya
- Speed It Up
- Thumbs Up/Thumbs Down
- Body Parts
- Flight

CALENDAR

MARCH
<u>On and Off Balance</u>
- Static/Dynamic
- Base of Support
- Counterbalancing
- Weight Bearing
- Balance Master
- Symmetry/Asymmetry
- Acro-Balance
- Partner Supports
- Wand-erful Balances
- Hit the Brakes

CALENDAR

APRIL
<u>Muscle Up</u>
- Pumping Rubber
- Above the Belt
- Power Pulls
- Repetitions
- Legs Only
- Resistance
- Tired Out
- Explode
- Iso Iso Iso
- Junkyard Gym

CALENDAR

MAY
<u>Striking</u>
- Hand Paddles
- Level Swing Plane
- Get Into the Swing
- Hit Parade
- Delivery Speed
- Keep It Up
- Arms Extended
- "Popping Can" Basics
- Touch
- Reaction Time

CALENDAR

JUNE
<u>Dance and Rhythms</u>
- Keep the Beat
- Twister
- Scattered Squares
- Copy Cat
- Stomp
- Dancing through the Decades
- Chair Dancing
- It's Electric
- The Beat Is On
- Points of Interest

CALENDAR

Pre-Sport Skills for Elementary Children—TAKE-HOME THEMES

SEPTEMBER
Working Together
- Alphabet Push-Ups
- Double Dribble
- Invent-a-Game
- Odd Ball
- Around the World
- Garbage Bag Basketball
- Cross Over
- Partner Support
- Ping-Pong Puff
- Move It

OCTOBER
Speed
- Scream Race
- Sprint Poles
- Drop the Pencil
- Jump the Tire
- Beat the Clock
- Jump Turns
- Penny Catch
- Fumble
- Fizzle
- Rubber Bounds

NOVEMBER
Offense and Defense
- Ace of Angles
- Power Balloon Volleyball
- Down Low
- Fake It 'Til You Make It
- Tiger Tales
- Homerun
- KOG
- Pancake
- Hands Up
- Two vs. One

DECEMBER
Mind and Muscle
- Sport Trading Card
- Wrong Number
- Prediction
- Color
- Compression and Tension
- Architecture
- Put on the Hat
- Absorption
- Color Run
- Couch Calisthenics

JANUARY
Heart Healthy
- Stronger Heart
- Pumping Rubber
- Box Out
- Shake the Snake
- Heart Partners
- Balloon Juggle
- Run the Block
- Anaerobic
- Cool It
- Save Those Beats

FEBRUARY
Sending and Receiving
- Penny Push
- Sock It to Me
- Sport Scoops
- Stairmaster
- Step Back
- Learning to Juggle
- Paper Plate Pennies
- Popping Cans
- High Flyers
- Target Practice

MARCH
On and Off Balance
- Jump George
- Power Pick-Up
- Counterbalancing
- TV Tasks
- Balance Masters
- Cupstack
- Push and Catch
- Doubles
- Balancing the Books
- Tai Chi

APRIL
Muscle Up
- Decathlon
- Couch Calisthenics
- Drawbridge
- Muscle Worm
- Soup Can Run
- Towel Pull
- King and Queen of Cards
- Tire Throw
- Wall Ball Curl-Ups
- Push-Up Hockey

MAY
Striking
- Kick-Off Can
- Foot Golf
- Homebowl
- Shoebox Derby
- Jumping-Jack Soccer
- Grocery Bag Dribble
- Sock-R-Cise
- Drop and Hit
- Soft Toss
- Nondominant Side

JUNE
Dance and Rhythms
- Wrist Dancing
- Grapevine
- Rhythmic Gymnastics
- Match This
- Stomp
- Juggling Plastic
- Invisible Ropes
- Ten
- Underlying Beat
- Chinese Jump Rope

Important Terms

To ensure student safety and understanding of the lesson content, the following terms are important for students and staff to know.

- *Aerobic* Aerobic activity is continuous and of long duration. Examples are jogging, rope skipping, and active games.

- *Cooperative* Cooperative activities encourage partners, and small and large groups to work together to solve a problem or attain a mutual goal.

- *General Space* General space is the total movement area of the room. It is often referred to as common space.

- *Inclusion* This is involvement in all activities regardless of the physical challenge through modification of the task, equipment, or space.

- *Integration* An interdisciplinary approach linking academic and movement skills. An example would be learning about the heart through negotiating a variety of heart-related functions (stations) on the gym floor.

- *Personal Space* This is the area around your body that you can touch when one body part is in contact with the floor.

- *Success-oriented* Success-oriented activities are movement tasks, drills, and games that remove the negative pressure existing in many traditional activities by motivating students to improve through positive reinforcement, rule adjustments, and multiple opportunities for success.

- *Theme* This is the central movement message or focus of the lesson.

CONTENTS

Part One

THE LESSONS

WORKING TOGETHER

A Gallup Poll surveyed 15,000 students, school personnel, and community members as to what was the most important thing to teach in physical education. Unanimously, each group selected the *ability to work together* as the most significant. The common theme in this monthly section is working together to achieve a common goal.

Alone we can do so little. Together we can do so much.

Contents

THREESOMES

WARM-UP

WATER–FIRE–TREES. Divide blue, red, and green vests, pinnies, or taped colored sheets among class members. Following a signal to begin, *water* (blue) players chase and attempt to tag *fire* (red) who tag only **trees** (green) who tag only **water**.

CONCEPT

Distribute a medicine ball, basketball, or large playground ball to each group of three. Find different ways to lift the ball using only your feet. All three of you must be in contact with the ball.

CHALLENGE

In groups of three, distribute one 2-gallon can to each person. Starting on one sideline, challenge each group to share cans as they attempt to cross the floor without stepping off the shared cans. A fourth can be added to simplify the crossing. ("Water Fire Tree." Courtesy of Dr. Lea Ann Martin, Western Washington University, Bellingham.)

CLOSER

Pass out one long jump rope (snake) to each group of three. With a turner on each end and a jumper in the middle, turners shake the rope as jumpers attempt to avoid touching the snake.

Name _____

Room _____

ALPHABET PUSH-UPS

Write out all of the letters in the alphabet. Cut out each letter and _spread_ them face up throughout your living room. Can you place them in order by moving only from a push-up position?

Opposing Forces

WARM-UP

Find a partner. Partner #1 sits with feet against the wall. Partner #2 stands next to #1 facing the opposite wall. Following a signal to begin, #1 raises feet up the wall—lifting his or her bottom off the ground—and holds until #2 touches the opposite wall and returns. Partners score collective points each time a partner is able to hold the wall position. Change places and continue for one to three minutes.

CONCEPT

Try these cooperative balances:

CHALLENGE

Hold hands, lean back, and change levels. How far back can you lean?

CLOSER

ODD AND EVEN CIRCLE.   Arrange students in a circle formation (hands held.) Number off each student: "one," "two," etc. Following a signal to begin, #1's lean in and #2's lean out, stabilizing the group.

Name _____

Room _____

DOUBLE DRIBBLE

For this activity you will need a partner, a clear flat surface, and two basketballs (or rubber playground or soccer balls). Once partners agree upon a destination, they grab inside hands and attempt to dribble to that spot.

Options:

- alternate sides
- exchange balls when moving
- one dribbles high while one dribbles low
- dribble backwards

HELPING HANDS

WARM-UP

TUNNEL TAG. Designate three students as taggers. The remaining class members run within the boundaries trying to avoid being tagged. Tagged individuals freeze on that spot assuming a standing position with legs spread wide apart. Non-tagged members free their frozen counterparts by crawling under their legs. Rescuers can give themselves a point for each individual they "save."

CONCEPT

Distribute one soccer ball, rubber playground ball, or basketball to each set of partners. **Can the two of you**:

- Sit down and stand up with a ball balanced between backs?
- Stand back to back and exchange a ball under one partner's legs and over heads (like a Ferris wheel)?
- Exchange a ball as you alternate sit-ups?

CHALLENGE

Place a ball between stomachs. Have partner #1 turn slowly to his or her right and partner #2 turn slowly in the same direction while maintaining pressure on the ball. If done correctly, the results will be one full rotation without losing the ball. Other body parts that also work include rotations with a ball between hips, chests, and foreheads.

CLOSER

HAND-TO-HAND HOOP PASS. Groups of 6–8 form a line and grab inside hands. The leader picks up a hula hoop, steps through, and lifts it over the second person's head. The second person (without letting go of hands) passes it down the line. How many hoops can you pass through the line in two minutes?

Name _____

Room _____

INVENT-A-GAME

Using the options of Space, Apparatus, Numbers, Game Type, and Formation below, create a new game never before played. Take at least one option from each area.

- **Space** (yard, field, house, court, etc.)
- **Apparatus** (racquet, bat, ball, net, etc.)
- **Numbers** (partners, trios, foursome, etc.)
- **Game Type** (tag, accuracy, 2 vs. 2, etc.)
- **Formation** (square, facing, spread, etc.)

Draw a picture of your invention below.

ONE STEP BACK

WARM-UP

SHADOWING.   Have students partner up and decide who will be #1 and #2. When the music is playing, #1 attempts to lose #2. Partner #2 stays as close as possible without tagging the chasee. When the music stops, *all* partners *freeze.* The chasers get one step to touch their partner. Partners reverse roles and the music starts again. Score one point for each "one step" tag.

CONCEPT

ACCURACY.   Place the same partners (facing) at mid-court. Distribute one beanbag or Nerf™ ball to each set of partners. Partner #1 hands the ball across and the receiver takes one step back. This process continues until a miss occurs. After a miss, both partners return to their starting positions. How far apart can you be? (**Teachers:** Emphasize accurate throws and two-handed catches.)

CHALLENGE

ONE-STEP BOWL.   Place a pin or empty 2-liter plastic bottle between partners and distribute one rubber playground ball or basketball. Partners alternate rolling the ball at the pin. Once a pin is knocked over, partners take one step back. The pin is reset and the game continues.

CLOSER

WALL PUSH-UPS.   Students face a clear wall, take a step back, fall forward, catch, and push back to a balance. They take a small step back after each success.

Name _____

Room _____

ODD BALL

Find a partner and a ball and try some of these cooperative challenges.

- Sit side by side (hip to hip) in a crab position and explore ways to transfer a ball from one lap to another.
- Stand back to back. As the ball is handed off overhead, the receiving partner returns it by passing under his or her legs. How fast can you move the ball?
- One partner sits (legs curled up) and the other stands (in front) with the ball. The standing partner tosses gently to the sitting partner who attempts to *pop* it back with his or her feet.
- What other ways can you move or pass a ball (feet only) up and down?

Cooperative Strength Training

WARM-UP

Stand facing a partner. Extend arms with one partner's hands on elbows and the other with back of hands on the inside. Practice pushing in and out. Try the same drill with legs while in a sitting position. What other cooperative pushes can you think of?

CONCEPT

Partners sit and face each other interlocking hands and sitting on each other's feet. Partner #1 pulls #2 up to a stand. When #2 comes back down, #1 comes up.

CHALLENGE

Partners face with hands held. Partner #1 stands and #2 sits. As #2 is pulled up, #1 sits. Which set of partners can perform 25 of these exercises in 60 seconds?

CLOSER

POPSICLE™ PUSH-UPS. Arrange students in the formation shown in the photo. Can your group perform a push-up while in this position?

Name _____

Room _____

AROUND THE WORLD

Find two partners and one basketball, volleyball, rubber playground ball, or soccer ball. See how many of the following stunts you can do without using your hands.

- **"360."** Hold hands and pass a ball with feet to each member of the group.
- How fast can you accomplish this?
- Change direction.

ONE-ON-ONE

WARM-UP

Find a partner. Partner #1 obtains a rubber playground ball. Both partners face in a sitting position. Place the ball between your feet and practice raising and lowering. Find three other positions where you can raise and lower. Can you move and keep the ball balanced?

CONCEPT

PUSH AND RESIST. Have partners try the following **push** and **resist** activities:

CHALLENGE

SCOOTER. Sit facing one another, grab hands, and place your feet under your partner's seat. Squeeze close together and practice rocking backward and forward. How many can travel across the floor while in this position?

CLOSER

Face each other (2 to 3 feet apart) in a baseball catcher's position. With palms forward and fingertips up, try to push/fake your partner off balance. **CAUTION:** No holding; just hand slaps and fakes.

Name _____

Room _____

Garbage Bag Basketball

To complete this activity, you will need a partner, a basketball goal, a large plastic garbage bag, and one basketball (or soccer ball or rubber playground ball).

The object is to throw the ball from the bag into the hoop. Partners stand just in front of the goal, place the ball in the middle of the bag, hold opposite ends, and fling the ball toward the hoop. As you become more accurate, try the following:

- How many can you make in 60 seconds?
- How many can you make in a row?
- How many can you make from 10 steps back?

Cooperative Challenges

WARM-UP

Divide the class in half and place at opposite ends of the gym or field. Distribute a flag, old tie, or 12-inch dust rag to one of the teams. You stand in the middle of the playing area and give a signal to begin, after which players without flags attempt to steal from opponents and deliver to you. Play in one-minute intervals. Teams must remain within established boundaries.

CONCEPT

Working in groups of three to four, try the following:
- Move across the floor using just three automobile tires.
- Make a basket while tossing a ball from a large plastic garbage bag.
- Join hands, place a ball between each player's ankles, and jump across the floor.
- Pass a Frisbee™ disc from one end of a line to the other using only your knees.

CHALLENGE

Place students in groups of four. Three form a triangle with hands held. The fourth student takes five steps back, calls the name of someone in the triangle, and then attempts to tag that player. Students in the triangle block the tagger with their arms by moving the target away from the tagger. (Triangles cannot run away from tagger.)

CLOSER

Arrange class members in single file. Have them close their eyes and try to rearrange themselves in alphabetical (first name) order.

Name _____

Room _____

CROSS OVER

For this activity all you need is a partner and some masking tape. Roll two strips of tape on a floor or carpet 10 feet long and 4 inches apart. The goal in this activity is for partners to pass each other touching opposite ends of the taped beam and return without stepping off. Find three different ways to cross over.

WITH HANDS HELD

WARM-UP

With hands held, do five push-ups, five jumping jacks, five standing long jumps, touch four walls, and give each other a high five.

CONCEPT

JUMP TOGETHER. Stand side by side with jump ropes held behind you. Exchange inside handles with your partner. Practice jumping forward and backward.

CHALLENGE

Distribute a ball to each person. With inside hands held, CAN YOU:
- Dribble and maintain control?
- Exchange balls and maintain control?
- Dribble at three different levels?

CLOSER

KNOTS. Arrange students in groups of 4 or 5 in a circle. Students shake right hands with one person across the circle and left hands with a different person. Once the knot is formed, individuals try to step in, around, and over each other attempting to **untie** the knot and return to a circular formation. Hands may turn but cannot be released.

Name _____

Room _____

PARTNER SUPPORT

Find a partner and stand toe to toe with fingers interlocked. Slowly lean back to a chair-sit position. Partners must work together so that they avoid sitting down. It takes cooperation for this to work!

FRIENDS TOGETHER

1 WARM-UP

Shake hands with a partner. For the next few minutes, you will do everything together. Sit facing, legs apart, toes touching, hands held. Partner #1 leans forward and #2 leans back. Try this slowly at first.

2 CONCEPT

Partner #1 closes his or her eyes while #2 vocalizes directions to a nearby location, e.g., door, mid-court, etc. After switching places, put one partner on a scooter. With slight pressure on shoulders, steer the partner safely through "traffic."

3 CHALLENGE

Place a balloon or beachball between heads while both partners attempt to:
- Do a hand clap routine.
- Touch the floor.
- Perform low jumps.
- Do a push-up.
- Turn in a circle.

4 CLOSER

Challenge another set of partners to see who can transport the most balloons across the room (without hands) in one minute. Transport as many as you can at a time. *If you were able to work together as friends during the lesson, there's a good chance you can do this forever!*

Name _____

Room _____

PING-PONG PUFF

For this activity you need two to four players and one ping-pong ball.

TWO PLAYERS:

Lie on stomachs. Players attempt to blow the ball back and forth, controlling its direction with gentle and forceful puffs of air.

THREE OR FOUR PLAYERS:

Lie on stomachs. With players forming a triangle or square, the goal is to move the ball (without letting it stop) from player to player. Can you do this from a push-up position?

TEAMWORK

 ## WARM-UP

ALL HANDS. In groups of five or more, set a team goal for jogging nonstop for one, two, or three minutes. Jogging is shoulder to shoulder with hands held. Once one person slows down, *all* slow down.

 ## CONCEPT

Distribute a large rubber playground ball to each team of four. Challenge students to discover a way to lift and hold a ball off the ground using only:
- fingertips
- heads
- feet

 ## CHALLENGE

ANIMAL FARM. Arrange students in open areas around the room. Students stand frozen with eyes closed. As you move by each student, touch their shoulder 1, 2, 3, or 4 times. 1 tap = DOG "bark"; 2 taps = SHEEP "baa"; 3 taps = COW "moo"; and 4 taps = DUCK "quack." Following the signal to begin, students move slowly about the room with palms up (eyes closed) while making the sound and attempting to chain up with the similar animals on their team.

 ## CLOSER

Teams sit in single file lines of 6–8. Members place legs over the thighs of the person in front. With hands to their sides, the last person (coxswain) calls "Stroke." Upon hearing this signal, all teammates lift their bottoms and push forward at the same time. Which team can remain intact and move 30 feet first?

Name _____

Room _____

MOVE IT

Gather all your family for this cooperative full-contact challenge. Select a clear space and designate start and finish lines. With each member connected, try to move the entire team from line to line while:

- arms are interlocked
- only one body part per person is on the ground
- one person is elevated off the ground (**BE CAREFUL!**)

WORKING TOGETHER

SEPTEMBER

SUNDAY	MONDAY	TUESDAY	WEDNESDAY	THURSDAY	FRIDAY	SATURDAY
Help a younger sibling or friend learn a new skill.	*(illustration)*	CHILDREN NEED MODELS MORE THAN THEY NEED CRITICS.		*(illustration)*	**S**tand facing a partner 2' away with palms out. Fall forward & catch each other. Push back to a balance. How far apart can you get?	**F**ind a jump rope & a partner. Can both of you jump the same rope?
While in contact, alternate sit-ups & push-ups with a partner.	**S**urprise someone with a good deed.	**F**ind a partner & place a long strip of tape on the floor. Can you pass each other without stepping off?	**W**ork cooperatively to learn & perform a new partner gymnastic stunt.	**I**nvent an exercise that moves a ball from partner to partner.	**F**ind a balloon & play a volleyball game over a chair.	**H**elp with a family meal and later work off those calories with a run.
With a partner, create a sliding dance on towels.	**H**ow many collective laps (add them together) can you & a friend run around the house in 15 minutes?	**G**o on a shadow run with a partner. Everywhere your partner jogs, you follow.	**P**lay a partner catching game with a ball. Each time you catch it take a step back	**T**each your family an activity you learned in P.E.	**D**o 3 or more special acts of kindness to different people at school.	**S**pend 30 minutes helping a neighbor. Name_____ Job_____
For 10 or more minutes, practice sending & receiving a ball with a family member or friend.	**T**hrow a knotted towel in the air and catch it cooperatively with a partner without using hands.	**C**reate a dance that includes lifting your partner.	**F**ind 4 people & form a circle. Shake right hands with someone across from you and left with a different person. Can you re-form a circle without releasing hands?	**S**hadow a partner dribbling a ball first with hands & second with feet.	**S**it back to back. Interlock arms; push against each other and try to stand up.	**O**rganize a family game.
Lie shoulder to shoulder; place inside arms over your partner's back & try to do a one-arm push-up.	**S**it back to back with a partner. Place a ball between your backs and try to turn around without dropping the ball.	**S**it facing a partner with legs apart. Hold hands; as one leans forward the other leans back.	**T**ake turns spotting each other's headstands or handstands.	**T**ie 2 bicycle inner tubes together & place around partner's waist. Begin a slow jog apart.	**P**lace an ice cube on your counter and do an exercise routine with a partner until it melts.	**S**it facing a partner. One partner's legs are inside & the other's outside. Practice squeezing in & out.

Calendar calisthenics is a voluntary daily fitness supplement conducted outside of school. As homework is completed, parents put a check in the corner box for the day. Small doses of creative

Name _____

Room _____

  Homework

Work together with your family to match the
clues and professional teams. Draw a line
connecting the clue to the appropriate team.

Clue	Team
solar discs	Washington Wizards
motor necessity	Indiana Pacers
royalty	Chicago Bulls
cow lovers	Cleveland Cavaliers
magical	Detroit Pistons
musical mode	Utah Jazz
gold-mine discovery	Houston Rockets
up-front runners	Sacramento Kings
dashing gentlemen	Phoenix Suns
New York chorus line	Denver Nuggets

Return to your P.E. Teacher

SPEED

"Nothing beats speed." It is essential to success in both team and individual sports. The focus this month will center around changing speeds, reaction time, and explosive actions.

In the race for quality, there is no finish line.
—David T. Kerns

Contents

Reflex

WARM-UP

This drill focuses on changing movements each time the whistle blows. Teach the following sequence. Blow the whistle every five seconds.
- Run in place "fast feet."
- Jog safely in "traffic."
- Run in place "fast feet."
- Jump touch toes; repeat.
- Run in place "fast feet."
- Side shuffle steps—side wall to side wall.

CONCEPT

PARTNER STEAL THE BACON.   Arrange partners on opposite end lines. Beanbags are placed between each pair on the mid-court line. Following the signal to begin, partners race to mid-court, pick up their bag, and attempt to return to the start line before being tagged. Give yourself **one** point each time you pick up the bag first and **two** points if you return safely.

CHALLENGE

CLAP 'n CATCH.   Distribute one rubber playground ball, soccer ball, or basketball to each set of partners. Partner #1 holds the ball on #2's back (just below the neck). Without warning, #1 drops the ball and #2 attempts to catch it from behind. Can anyone clap their hands in front before catching? Trade places after every **three** turns.

CLOSER

PARTNER BEANBAG STEAL.   Partners face in a cross-legged (sitting) position with a beanbag between. Hands are placed on thighs. When I call "left hand," "right hand" or "both hands," try to be the first to pick up the bag with the correct body part. Who can score 10 points first?

Name _____

Room _____

SCREAM RACE

Many years ago, Native Americans living around the Northwest beaches would increase their lung capacity by taking a deep breath and exhaling with a loud "aaaahhhhhh" as they ran down the beach. Not only was this exhilarating, but it also kept them fit.

With your family or small group of friends, choose a starting spot on a sidewalk or open field. Take a deep breath and run as fast and far as you can without taking a second breath. Once you run out of breath, stop and stand on that spot. Who can go the farthest on a single breath?

Quick Feet

WARM-UP

PARTNER STEP UP.   Place 4′ × 8′ or 5′ × 10′ foldable mats around the floor and arrange partners on opposite sides of the mats. Following a signal to begin, students step up and down as fast as they can for rounds of 30, 60, and 90 seconds. Next, have students select a number of step ups, e.g., 25, 30, 40, etc., and see which partner can attain that number of steps first. (**Note:** Most 4′ × 8′ mats will allow four people ample room to work.)

CONCEPT

WHISTLE SPRINTS.   Place cones around the room to form an oval running track. Students start jogging counterclockwise. Each time you blow the whistle, they sprint as fast as they can until they hear the next whistle. Between whistles (3-second intervals) students simply walk or jog.

CHALLENGE

DON'T STEP ON MY TOES.   Select partners and find an open space. Interlock fingertips. When you say "GO" see if the partners can touch each other (with toes) 10 times before the other partner makes 10 contacts. Vocalize each contact: "one," "two," "three," etc.

CLOSER

CATCH ME IF YOU CAN.   Students form a large circle, number off "1," "2," "3," etc., and lie down (heads toward center). Following your signal to begin, #1 jumps up, begins running counterclockwise around the circle, and returns to the starting position. As soon as #1 is on her or his feet, #2 goes. This process continues until everyone has run and is back in the lying position. **Option:** Time the group.

Name _____

Room _____

Take Home

SPRINT POLES

Telephone or light poles provide an excellent venue for practicing sprints. World-class sprinters have been clocked at more than 22 miles per hour. Ask a friend or family member to count the number of seconds it takes you to sprint from one pole to another. Count "one thousand one, one thousand two," etc.

Options
- Race a friend.
- Reduce the number of steps between poles.
- Improve your previous <u>best</u> time.

ACCELERATE

WARM-UP

BUMBLEBEE TAG.   Designate two to three students as taggers. Taggers carry foam stingers (pieces of pipe insulation) and attempt to tag (sting) as many runners as possible in 60 seconds. Tagged runners freeze and **raise one hand.** Any non-tagged runner can *free* stung runners with a high-five. ("Chuk-em." Courtesy of Chuck and Barb McEwan.)

CONCEPT

COUNTDOWN.   Distribute one jump rope to each student. As you count down "10," "9," "8"—students jump faster and faster until "1" is called. Remember, start slow and end fast.

CHALLENGE

Distribute one basketball or bouncy playground ball to each student. When you say "Go," students dribble in control to the opposite wall and back three times. On the first trip, dribble slowly. On the second trip, bounce the ball a bit faster. On the final trip, bounce as fast as possible without losing control.

CLOSER

LINE-UP.   Arrange students in specific spots (lines, circle, etc.). When you say "Go," students line up behind you as fast as possible according to:
- height
- alphabetical (first name)
- birthday, etc.

Name _____

Room _____

DROP THE PENCIL

Partners face one step apart. Partner #1 holds an unsharpened pencil chest high. Partner #2, with hands at sides, attempts to catch the dropped pencil with **two** hands before it hits the ground. Allow ten turns per partner. Who had the better score?

If you were able to catch at least five, see if you can catch the object with **one** hand.

My best score was _____ out of ten.

CHARGE

WARM-UP

Using an indoor or outdoor baseball diamond, place half the class 10 feet behind second base and the remaining half in a single line 10 feet behind home plate. On "Go," the first runner from each line sprints counterclockwise around the bases touching each base along the way. Every three seconds, a whistle will blow signaling the next runner in each line to start. The runner's goal is to try to touch the person ahead of him or her. After the last base is touched, runners move quickly to the end of their respective line. Which line can complete the relay first? <u>Tagged runners continue to run.</u>

CONCEPT

Arrange students 15–20 feet back from a clear wall. Distribute one rubber tennis or racquet ball per student. Challenge students to practice throwing the ball off the wall and catching the rebound. Can students catch the rebound without moving their feet? Class members able to accomplish this skill should be further challenged to **<u>charge</u>** the rebounds attempting to catch their ball in as few bounces as possible.

CHALLENGE

Can you catch your ball before it bounces three times? Two? How far back can you move and remain accurate? Partner up and practice charging each other's rebounds.

CLOSER

BOUNCE AND JUMP.   **Find a clear open** space and bounce your ball as high as you can. How many times can you *jump* over it before it comes to rest? Next, how many times can you get *under* your bounce?

Name _____

Room _____

JUMP THE TIRE

For this activity, you will need a small automobile tire and a safe open space. Practice rolling the tire and see how many times you can jump over it (without touching) before it comes to a stop.

On Your Mark, Get Set, Go!

WARM-UP

This lesson works best on a playground or large open field. Arrange students in a large circle formation. Following your signal to begin, students jog in place, lifting their knees (thighs parallel to the ground). Try this for 30 seconds. "Ready?" "Go." During the next 30 seconds, continue with the high knees while moving arms up and down <u>rapidly.</u> Try to keep wrists and fingertips loose. Next, have students face outside of the circle and, on "Go," let students apply these principles as they perform a high knee rapid arm swing away from the circle.

CONCEPT

Find a partner. Agree upon a distance away from the start line and place one ball down. "On your mark": Partners place both hands behind the line with the dominant leg forward and opposite knee resting on the ground. "Set": Hips are raised. "Go": Race to the designated mark. Repeat three times.

CHALLENGE

FIVE-SECOND SPRINT. Arrange students on a single starting line and distribute one tennis ball per student. If space is cramped, number off students #1, #2, and allow half the class to run at a time. On "Go," students sprint as fast as possible for *five seconds*. After you call "FREEZE," students stop, place, and leave their tennis ball at that point. On the second round, students try to run past their original mark. Encourage students to spread out and run in straight pathways.

CLOSER

SHUTTLE RUN. Place two lines of four facing 20–30 yards apart. Runner #1 from line one begins by running and transferring a baton to the first person in the opposite line. This process continues until each runner is back in his or her original position. Runners move to the end of the opposite line.

Name _____

Room _____

Take Home

BEAT THE CLOCK

To complete this activity you need a clear area, a partner, one tennis ball or small rubber ball, and three containers (wastebasket, boxes, etc.).

Place the containers on either a line or in a scattered formation. The thrower stands 10 or more feet away from the target. A second person serves as the timer.

How many seconds does it take to _bounce_ your ball into all three of the containers? The thrower retrieves each ball and returns to the throwing line for succeeding throws.

My best time was _____ seconds.

Slo Mo

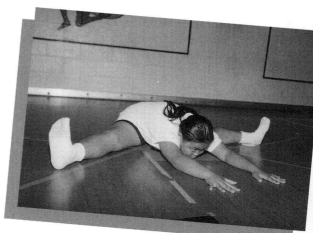

WARM-UP

From a sitting position, legs apart, place your hands on your knees and S-L-O-W-L-Y move them toward your toes, lowering your chest at the same time.

CONCEPT

SLO RACE.   Arrange students on one sideline. When you say "Go," students move as slowly as possible (without stopping) to the opposite wall. Return moving backwards in slow motion. Next, students move across the floor according to the signals you give them. **Two hands** mean sprint; **one hand** means jog; and **arms folded** means slow motion.

CHALLENGE

You tape a sporting event on television. The program should be action oriented (boxing, basketball, karate, etc.). Show the recorded video and have students mimic portions of the tape at regular speed. Next, put the proceedings in slo mo and ask students to mirror these movements as well.

CLOSER

RED LIGHT—GREEN LIGHT.   Align students on one sideline. When you say "green light," they *creep* forward slowly until they hear you say "red light." Those students caught moving on "red light" must return to the starting line and begin moving on the next "green light." Let's see how many of you can make it across without getting caught. *Variation:* Hold up colors.

Name _____

Room _____

JUMP TURNS

Speed and jumping ability are essential skills to becoming a successful athlete. For the following drill you need a partner and a clear space. Partners face each other and decide who will jump and turn first. Partner #1 jumps and attempts to make a full rotation. Partner #2 then tries to match or surpass this effort. Each time partners accomplish a full rotation, they give each other "high fives." Once you get the hang of it, try the following:

- Jump at the same time.
- Try to land at the same time.
- Turn in opposite directions.

What was more important, jumping higher or turning faster?

Jump City

WARM-UP

(**Teacher:** Compare the painted maze of lines on the gym floor to a video game screen.) Have students pretend they are a character from the game Pac Man.™ The only way one can escape the ghosts is to run and jump from line to line. Students tagged or caught off a line must move to the middle of the floor and perform a penalty, e.g., toss and catch a beanbag 10 times before reentering. Two taggers (wearing vests or pinnies) serve as ghosts.

CONCEPT

HUMAN HURDLES. Mark off a large running oval in or outside the gym. Place a set of partners in the north, south, east, and west quadrants of the room. Partners assume foot position "A." Class members run and jump the human hurdles in a counterclockwise direction. Jumpers touching a hurdle take that person's place. Runners complete 2–5 laps before elevating hurdles to positions "B" and "C."

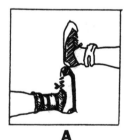
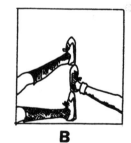
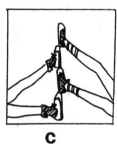

A **B** **C**

CHALLENGE

Using the formations described above, establish two lines and have the first two students in line **race each other** over each hurdle. Once a lap is completed, runners slap hands with the new line leaders and move to the end of the line. *Variation:* Run lines in opposite directions.

CLOSER

HOOP JUMP. Distribute one hoop to each set of partners. Partner #1 holds the hoop at low, medium, and high levels while #2 attempts to jump inside.

Take Home

PENNY CATCH

Here's a great idea for improving your speed and reaction time. Place your dominant hand (palm down) so that your thumb touches the lobe of your ear. Your forearm now forms a flat surface. Place a penny on this surface, drop your hand, and attempt to catch the falling penny.

If you are successful catching a single penny, try stacking two or more!

My penny-catching record was _____.

PACE

1 WARM-UP

This lesson is best suited for outdoors. A pace is the distance between steps and also the speed of those steps. Let's see if students can keep pace on a 200- to 300-yard jog. Form a single line leaving a 3- to 5-foot space between each runner. Can they jog the course without stopping? Passing?

2 CONCEPT

STRIDE LENGTH. Space four cones evenly around the same course. Start jogging using short quick steps. Each time students pass a cone, they increase the length of their stride. What stride length allowed you to cover the most ground the fastest?

3 CHALLENGE

Challenge a partner to a leap-for-distance contest. Using a running approach, take off from a predetermined line. To find out how far you have jumped, measure the distance between the takeoff line and the point where your back heel touches.

4 CLOSER

Experiment with changing the stride length of various locomotor movements (skip, hop, etc.). Start with short strides and gradually stretch them out.

Name _____

Room _____

FUMBLE

For this activity you need three people, a clear grassy area, and a football. Player #1 stands with the football. The other two players stand on opposite sides. The passer rolls the ball between the two receivers who attempt to gain control of the ball. The first to pick it up scores ONE point.

The passer rolls five balls before rotating to one of the receiver positions.

Options:
- Have the player gaining possession first try to run over a line without being tagged.
- Change rolls to balls thrown in the air or kicked.

Get a Clue

WARM-UP

BREAK THE TAPE. Number off in groups of four. Have #1 and #2 hold a 5-foot strip of masking tape or yarn. Team members #3 and #4 race short distances to see who can break the tape first. Alternate runners and holders after each race.

CONCEPT

CLUE. Select five names of current famous NBA, NFL, or MLB players. Place each name on a separate card and hide around the playground. Issue each student a card containing clues to locate the five hidden names. Once a name is found, students record it next to the appropriate clue. Students are encouraged to sprint to each location.

> **SAMPLE:** (Clue) "Don't get <u>tired</u> out." (LOCATION) Playground truck tire. (NAME) Ken Griffey, Jr.

CHALLENGE

PRIVATE NUMBER. Place sets of partners around the perimeter of the gym and scatter 30 index cards face down in the middle of the floor. Each card has a number from 1 to 30. Partners are assigned one private number. Following a signal to begin, partner #1 sprints out and picks up one card. If the card selected does not have his or her private number, it is placed back (face down) and that runner returns to tag partner #2. This process continues until both of their numbers are found.

CLOSER

Distribute score cards to each student listing permanent objects found around the playground. The majority of large playground apparatus has a brand name. The goal of the runner is to locate and record that name. How fast can you copy a key word and return with all the blanks filled in?

> **SAMPLE:** Slide—Made in USA
> Light Pole—*City Light*
> Gate—No motorized vehicles

Name _____

Room _____

FIZZLE

For this activity you will need a deflated balloon and a clear space. "Fizzle" tests your speed and reaction time. Simply blow up the balloon (to about the size of a cantaloupe), hold it above your head, and release. How many times out of ten can you catch the flying object *before* it hits the ground?

Challenge another family member to a catching contest. Do NOT share balloons. Remember to keep balloons away from very young children.

PURSUIT

WARM-UP

HOOP PURSUIT.   Divide the class into three groups and arrange in the locations shown below. Distribute a hula hoop to each player on the two sidewalls (A and B). On "GO," place hoops on the ground and slide them with their feet at students running down the middle. Runners from the end wall (group C) attempt to move to the opposite wall without being touched by a hoop. Allow 15 seconds before changing places. Players score a point for each hoop contact and each safe passage. Sliders receive one attempt per rotation. Replace hoops and rotate clockwise.

A ○○○○○
C-Runners →
○○○○○ B

CONCEPT

CLOTHESPIN TAG.   Divide the class in half. Designate one group as RED and the other as BLUE. One color-coded clothespin is placed in the middle of each player's back. A team bucket is situated on opposite endlines. On "GO" players attempt to take one pin at a time from an opponent and deposit it in their bucket. The team with more pins after two minutes scores the first point. (*Credit: Great Activities* newsletters, Nov./Dec. 1994, vol. 13, no. 2, p. 21.) (**Note:** Plastic pins are more durable than the wooden variety.)

CHALLENGE

PLAYGROUND BALL PURSUIT.   Distribute two playground balls to each set of partners. Designate partners as either #1 or #2. Partner #1 rolls his or her ball 30–40 feet across the floor, runs, and stands behind it. Partner #2 rolls and attempts to contact the stationary ball. Players alternate rolls until a ball is hit. The player making the first hit rolls the next ball. Encourage partners to run after their ball.

CLOSER

GET DOWN ON IT.   Partners find an open space and place a hula hoop between them. As music is played, partners skip counterclockwise around their hoop. When the music stops, the first partner to sit down inside scores a point. (*Teacher:* Stop the music every 10–15 seconds and change locomotor skills.)

Name _____

Room _____

RUBBER BOUNDS

While some may not associate rubber bands with improving physical skills, there are some activities that require speed and reaction time.

Find a rubber band and lie on the floor in a room with a low ceiling. Can you shoot the band off the ceiling and catch the rebound while remaining in a supine position?

Options: <u>CAN YOU</u>
- catch with the opposite hand?
- catch five in a row?
- catch on a different body part, e.g., stomach? legs? bottom of feet?

SPEED

OCTOBER

SUNDAY	MONDAY	TUESDAY	WEDNESDAY	THURSDAY	FRIDAY	SATURDAY
Face a partner, grab hands & see who can touch the other's feet with his or her feet 10 times first.	**W**hile watching TV, practice push-ups, attempting to clap your hands on the **PUSH-UP**.	**H**ave someone hold a small ball out in front of you. See if you can catch 5 of 10 balls dropped without warning.	*Find some stairs. Go up fast & down slowly. Repeat for each year you are old.*	**H**ow fast can you move a ball **BACK & FORTH** between your right and left foot?	*Play a game of push-tag with a family member. The first to touch the other's hand 10 times wins.*	**F**ind 2 trees or poles some 20 yards apart. Practice sprinting between the two.
How fast can you move your feet? When standing in one place, can you touch the floor 100 times in 60 seconds?	**T**ake a bouncy ball & practice bouncing it as fast as you can without losing control.	**P**lace a basketball, soccer ball, or large rubber ball in front of you. Alternate toe taps on top.	*Find a clear, grassy area & work on increasing your backward & lateral speed.*	**H**ave someone roll a ball out in front of you while you try to beat it to a line.	**C**hallenge someone in your neighborhood to a series of short & long races.	**C**an you jump & click your heels together? Can you click them twice in the air?
Olympic runners practice running steps with HIGH KNEES. How high can your knees be when you run?	**S**ee how fast you can transfer a small ball or beanbag from hand to hand.	**B**alance a small ball on your head. Lean forward & catch it in front. How many can you do in a row?	**B**ounce a ball & before the second bounce, clap hands & catch. • Touch floor & catch. • Sit on floor & catch. • Lie on floor & catch.	**T**oss a small ball upward with PALM UP & catch it with PALM DOWN. Try with each hand.	**H**ow quickly can you stack six plastic or paper cups in a 3–2–1 pyramid?	**F**ind someone with a watch & have him or her time you as you run around your house.
Play a tag game in a small space.	**M**ost sidewalks are 3 squares wide. Picture yourself as an Olympic sprinter & practice running in your lane.	**T**hrow a Frisbee™ or small ball a distance that requires you to run & catch it.	*Find a clear space to run & see how LONG your STRIDE can be when sprinting.*	**U**sing a real or imaginary jump rope, see how many jumps you can perform in 10 seconds.	*Roll 2 socks up in a tight ball. How long does it take to dribble (foot) into every room of your house?*	**C**an you JUMP & touch both toes when legs are pointed forward (pike)? Apart (straddle)?
Find a partner. Place 2 empty soft-drink cans 30' away from each person. Who can bring his or her can back first?	*Find a clear area & practice your bat speed. You can use nearly any type of stick. How fast is your swing?*	**P**ut a soup can in each hand & move them up, down, out & in as you jog around the block.	**I**t is better to fail at doing something than succeed in doing nothing.			

Calendar calisthenics is a voluntary daily fitness supplement conducted outside of school. As homework is completed, parents put a check in the corner box for the day. Small doses of creative

Name _____

Room _____

Ball Drop—Reaction Drill

Partner #1 stands behind Partner #2 holding a basketball against Partner #2's neck. Partner #2 stands with hands on thighs. Without warning, Partner #1 releases the ball and Partner #2 attempts to clap his or her hands (in front) prior to catching the ball behind. How many claps can you make before catching?

Return to your P.E. Teacher

OFFENSE AND DEFENSE

Activities in this section stress footwork, stances (hands-up), take-away skills, agility work, shielding, and guarding.

Offense, defense it changes in a heartbeat. Know the difference.

Contents

QUICK AS A CAT

1 WARM-UP

Select a partner and face each other on opposite sides of a line. One partner extends hands palms down while the second partner <u>links fingers</u> with palms up. Following a signal to begin, partners try to touch their opponents' toes with their toes *vocalizing* each contact. The first player to make 10 contacts wins the game. At no time may players release grips.

2 CONCEPT

EARTHQUAKE. Success in sports often depends upon a player's quickness. Students find a personal space and assume a slight crouch position with hands up. On "GO," they run (in place) as fast as they can move their feet. When you point to a direction, students maintain their defensive posture and *slide* in that direction.

3 CHALLENGE

SIDE SLIDE. Students select a new partner and face each other from opposite side walls. When you say "GO," see if they can slide step to their partner's wall and back before the partner can do the same. Remember, <u>**stay low, slide steps only, no crossovers.**</u> On the following rotations:
- leap across and back
- move backward across and back
- gallop across and back

4 CLOSER

BODY PART TAG. Designate 5–7 taggers, select a target body part (shoulders, hips, elbows, etc.), and start the game. Students who are tagged on the correct part hold that part with a free hand. Change parts every 60 seconds. Emphasize quick feet.

Name _____

Room _____

ACE OF ANGLES

For this activity you will need a rubber playground ball or soccer ball, a clear wall space, and one empty 2-liter plastic bottle.

Place the bottle six feet from the wall. Stand to the side of the bottle, kick the ball (side of foot), and see how many attempts it takes to strike the bottle when the ball rebounds off the wall. Each time you are successful, move a step to your right or left and experiment with a new angle.

To be the "Ace of Angles" you must hit _three in a row_ from 10 feet left or right of the bottle.

WARM-UP

Keeping your hands up on defense is an important defensive strategy. Have students find a *personal* space and assume the following defensive stance: (keep low, use slide steps, feet slightly wider than shoulders. Students are to watch your hand. When you point to a direction, students try to *shuffle* in that direction without crossing their feet.

CONCEPT

Form four separate lines on one endline. Place one ball at the head of each line. Line leaders (defenders) step out and face their line assuming an almost *sitting* defensive position. The second person dribbles a ball forward at a slow pace. The defender moves with hands up *without* stealing the ball. After arriving at the opposite wall, players switch roles and return moving to the end of their line. The next two players in line step forward and the process is repeated. Once the drill is understood, have students pick up the pace and move from sideline to sideline.

CHALLENGE

Students find a partner of similar height. Obtain one tennis ball. Partners alternate tossing the ball forcibly downward between the both of them and see who can obtain possession first. As they jump for the rebound, they must remember to keep their **hands up.**

CLOSER

Have students face a wall and reach up as high as possible. (**Teacher:** Place a sticker or small piece of tape one foot above their fingertips). On the "GO" signal, students jump, try to touch above their mark, rotate to the right, and repeat as they attempt to touch all of the other spots.

Name _____

Room _____

Power Balloon Volleyball

For this activity you will need a clear space in your house, a piece of furniture to serve as a net, one large 11-inch balloon, and a partner.

The game begins with one partner serving over the net. The receiving partner bumps, sets, and spikes (no more than three contacts) the balloon back over the makeshift net.

Options:

- Play a cooperative game. (Count the consecutive contacts.)
- Play a competitive game to 15 points.

PASS IT

1 WARM-UP

ALTERNATING BALLOON VOLLEY.
Select partners and distribute
one balloon per set. Scatter hula
hoops across the floor. Following
a signal to begin, students
alternate the balloon (bumps,
sets, passes) as they move from
hoop to hoop. Students select
their own penalty if the
balloon touches the floor or is
hit twice in a row
by the same person.

2 CONCEPT

PENNY PUSH.   Partners face on opposite sides of a line 6–10 feet apart.
Distribute one basketball or rubber playground ball to each set of partners.
Place a penny on the line. Demonstrate a chest bounce pass and challenge
partners to move the penny *toward* their partner by hitting it on the pass.

3 CHALLENGE

Partners form a square (10–12 feet apart) and count off #1 to #4. Instruct
teams to pass in the following pattern (#1 to #2; #2 to #3; #3 to #4) and
repeat. After completing three passes, they sit down. Next, try this drill passing
with their feet. Add additional rotations. Which group can sit down first?

4 CLOSER

SNAP BACK.   Using the same groups of four, arrange students in a single line
just two feet apart. Distribute one Nerf™ football per group. Partner #1 bends
down and hands the ball to #2 between his or her legs and runs to the end of
the line. #2 centers to #3 and the process repeats itself until the entire team
moves across the floor (backward toward the goal line). Dropped snaps are
repeated by the same person.

Name _____

Room _____

DOWN LOW

Find a bouncy ball. Using a wrist–fingertip action, practice bouncing your ball as low as you can when you are:

- standing
- on the move
- kneeling
- sitting
- using your nondominant hand
- bouncing from hand to hand
- lying on your back

TAKE-AWAYS

1 WARM-UP

Divide the class in half and place at opposite ends of the floor or field. Distribute flags, ties, strips of cloth, etc., to one team. Flags are placed at the hip or back pocket area; a player's only defense is outrunning the chaser. Once a flag is captured, the defender returns it to you, (stationed at midfield). When seven flags have been collected, teams switch places. An option is to time each team.

2 CONCEPT

Select partners and distribute one basketball or rubber playground ball per set. Following a signal to begin, the students with the ball begin dribbling in their personal space while the defender simply tries to touch the ball. Change possession after each touch. Additional space can be added as proficiency increases.

3 CHALLENGE

Facing partners sit cross-legged (one foot apart) with hands on knees. A beanbag is placed between partners. You provide the following vocal cues: "right," "left," or "both." Once the direction is called, players try to be the first to pick up the bag. A legal pickup scores one point for that player. The game can also be started with hands on different body parts (i.e., hands on shoulders).

4 CLOSER

Distribute one Nerf™ football or soccer ball to each group of three. Number off students #1, #2, and #3. Players #1 and #2 play catch while #3 attempts to intercept. Participants change places every 30 seconds.

Name _____

Room _____

Fake It Until You Make It

Locate a clear open space in your backyard or neighborhood park. Find a partner with whom to play offense and defense. Once you have agreed upon common boundaries, the game can begin.

Partners face at opposite ends of the playing area. The designated offensive player attempts to fake his or her way past the defensive player without being tagged. Players alternate positions after each run.

BEAT THE CLOCK

1 WARM-UP

SPEED. When you say "GO," in 60 seconds see if students can:
- Touch the side walls 10 times (back and forth).
- Catch a tennis ball (off a wall) 10 times from 15 feet back.
- Complete 15 push-ups.
- Give their team members five high-fives.
- When finished, *sit down.*

2 CONCEPT

During the next five minutes tell students they will attempt to complete each of the following five stations. As soon as they finish a task, they move quickly to their right and start the next.
- Jump rope 20 times.
- Shoot and make three baskets.
- Dribble a ball through an eight-cone obstacle course three times.
- Step up and down on a mat 50 times.
- Complete 15 sit-ups.

3 CHALLENGE

BEAT YOUR BEST SCORE. In 60 seconds set a:
- cumulative jumping jack record
- basketball bounce record
- soccer ball record (number of toe taps on top)

4 CLOSER

In 60 seconds, how many times can students . . . stand up, lie flat on their back, and stand up again? Students *count out loud* each time they come to a standing position.

Name _____

Room _____

TIGER TAILS

For this activity, you need a partner, an 18-inch strip of cloth (tie, dust cloth, etc.) and a clear open space. Partners hang their tails at waist level from back pockets, belts, or pants.

Players face each other from opposite sides of the playing area. One partner is designated as offense and one as defense. The defensive player calls "GO" and the offensive player attempts to run past the defense without losing his or her tail. Offense and defense alternate turns. Score a point for each successful run.

Players <u>may not</u> protect their tail by holding it or blocking the defensive player's hand.

DODGE CITY

1 WARM-UP

QUICK PACE IN A SMALL SPACE. Arrange students in personal space on one half of the floor. Remind them to move slowly at first and quicken the pace only when proficiency allows. The only rule when moving is they can't touch anyone else. They can begin by jogging and changing directions each time someone comes into their path. How long can they move without touching?

2 CONCEPT

CATCH ME IF YOU CAN. This activity is best suited for a large field. After students partner up, have them decide who will be the *chaser* and who will be the *chasee.* Once this is determined, a signal is given and the chasee flees (dodging, faking, changing directions), attempting to escape the shadow. After 30–60 seconds, players change places. A point is given for each legal tag. Remember to stay within the boundaries.

3 CHALLENGE

3 vs. 1 TAG. Have students arrange themselves in groups of four and number off "1," "2," "3," and #4. #'s 1–3 grab hands and form a triangle. #4 stands outside and calls the name of a player inside. Once the target is named, the triangle moves and attempts to block #4 from tagging the designated person. Triangle players can block with their arms and rotate the target away from the tagger. Once a person is tagged or 30 seconds elapses, a new tagger is selected.

4 CLOSER

In groups of three, have two players kneel or stand 8–10 feet apart. The third player stands in the middle and attempts to dodge the ball rolled between the partners. Once the ball touches that target, a new player moves to the middle.

Name _____

Room _____

Homerun

This activity provides an opportunity to increase one's offensive striking ability. Find a suitable ball and a plastic, wood, or metal bat (a broomstick will do). Place five markers 10–15 feet apart in a straight line.

Standing behind the first marker, self toss the ball and strike it over as many markers as possible. Students unable to self toss and hit can use batting tees. Hits clearing the second marker count as *singles;* the third, *doubles;* the fourth, *triples;* and the *fifth,* a *homerun.*

FOOT POWER

WARM-UP

This lesson is best suited for a large field. Distribute one rubber playground ball, soccer ball, or Nerf™ soccer ball to each student sitting throughout a general space. (Demonstrate punting a ball upward and catching it in as few bounces as possible.) How many of them are able to kick and catch a ball before it hits the ground?

CONCEPT

Students find a partner. Place one ball away and place the other at mid-field. In this activity students may only kick the ball the partners start with. Have partner #1 take one step back from the ball while #2 retreats some 15–20 yards away. Partners alternate kicks, attempting to be the first to kick it past their opponents' designated endline. Once the ball crosses the line, the game stops and the ball is returned to midfield with the nonscoring partner taking the next kick. Strategies should include kicking deep and utilizing angles to drive the ball past an opponent. (See the Take Home activity KOG on the next page.)

CHALLENGE

Place two large truck inner tubes at mid-field. Mark one tube blue and the other red. Situate groups of 4–6 behind each tube. Following a signal to begin, teams kick their tube toward an established goal line. As soon as the tube crosses the line, that team rolls it back to mid-field where another team awaits the start signal.

CLOSER

"500." Partners share one ball and alternate kicking to each other with an upward trajectory. Balls caught in the air are worth 100 points; one-bounce catches are 75 points; two-bounce catches are 50 points; and three- (or more) bounce recoveries are 25 points. How many kicks does it take to score 500 points? Play competitively or cooperatively.

Take Home

This stands for Kick Over Goal. For this activity you will need two people, a football, (or soccer ball or rubber playground ball), and an open football or soccer field. The object of the game is to be the first to kick the ball over an opponent's goal line.

The game begins with partner #1 kicking off from midfield. Partner #2 catches or traps the kick as quickly as possible and immediately tries to kick it past #1. An offensive strategy is to try to angle kicks toward a sideline, not allowing the receiver to stop the roll. Balls kicked out of bounds are rekicked from that point. Once a goal is scored, the defensive player receives the first kick.

VOLLEYING

1 WARM-UP

Volleying is striking the ball before it hits the ground. Provide music for this activity. Place a variety of objects (beachballs, Nerf™ balls, soccer balls, plastic balls with paddles, etc.) inside hoops in locations all around the room. On the "GO" signal, students skip, hop, gallop, and slide about the floor to the music. When the music stops, class members run to the closest hoop and volley any object from the hoop until the music begins again.

2 CONCEPT

Distribute one paddle/racquet and tennis ball per student. In their personal (self) space, see if students can balance their ball on the face of the paddle. Can they keep the ball balanced while walking across the floor? Can they bounce it off the face three times in a row? Off a wall? Start with a bounce and practice some wall volleys.

3 CHALLENGE

In groups of three, grab hands and form a triangle. Once all students are in the correct formation, distribute one large 11-inch balloon per team. Using forearms, heads, and knees, see how long the trio can volley the balloon without letting it hit the ground. Remember, hands must be held at all times.

4 CLOSER

Arrange two sets of partners (facing) across a line. Distribute one large plastic garbage bag per pair and one round Nerf™ ball for each foursome. How many consecutive volleys can your teams exchange from the stretched-out bags?

Name _____

Room _____

PANCAKE

The pancake catch is one of the surest methods of catching a Frisbee.™ To perform this catch, form a "V" with the heel of both hands and simply bring the fingers together as the object reaches the hands. Try this method when:

- Self tossing a Frisbee™ in the air.
- Receiving a Frisbee™ from a partner while stationary.
- Receiving a Frisbee™ while on the move.

SHIELDING

1 WARM-UP

Students face a partner and place both hands on each other's shoulders. When you say "GO," see who can get behind their partner first (bear-hug position). Students give themselves a point each time they are successful.

2 CONCEPT

Using the same partner, number off #1, #2. Distribute one ball per set. Partner #1 holds the ball and #2 lines up directly behind. (**Teacher:** Demonstrate shielding: *using your body to protect the ball.*) Following a signal to begin, #1 attempts to bounce and shield the ball from #2. Partner #2's goal is to touch the ball. When this occurs, the two change places. Next, try this skill when dribbling with the feet.

3 CHALLENGE

TWO vs. ONE. Place students in groups of three. This time, two opponents attack the ball. The player in possession tries to maintain control for 30 seconds. Switch places every 30 seconds. Remember, **no contact**.

4 CLOSER

Determine whether the class will dribble with hands or feet. Distribute balls to one-third of the class. Explain that if you have a ball, use good dribbling and shielding techniques to keep it. If you don't have a ball, try to take one away by touching just the ball.

Name _____

Room _____

HANDS UP

To complete this activity, you need three people, a bouncy ball, and an open space. Number off each partner (1–3). Partner #1 stands between #2 and #3 with hands up. The outside players attempt to pass the ball back and forth without the middle person intercepting. Passers must remain stationary while receivers can catch the ball while moving. As soon as the middle partner touches the ball, he or she takes the thrower's place. How many passes can you complete in a row?

WARM-UP

STAY CLOSE.   Distribute one playground ball to each set of partners. Partner #2 stands behind partner #1 and holds a ball on his or her back. Play music. After the music begins, both partners jog safely through "traffic" attempting to keep the ball on the leader's back. Change leaders every 30 seconds.

CONCEPT

Try the following partner and small group guarding situations:
- Two partners take turns kicking a *soft* ball at a guarded (taped) wall target.
- Three partners sit on their knees in a triangular formation. Place a pin in front of each player. Trio members roll a ball attempting to knock over other players' pins while blocking their own.

CHALLENGE

Partners hold inside hands. Partner #1 dribbles a basketball with his or her outside hand while #2 attempts to steal it. Remember, inside hands must be held. Switch ball handlers every 30 seconds.

CLOSER

LARGE FIELD TOUCHDOWN.   Team #1 stands on one end line. Each player displays a 12-inch flag, tie, or strip of cloth at belt level. Flags should not be tied to clothing. Team #2 spreads across the playing area about midfield. On "GO," Team #1 attempts to cross the opposite endline without losing its flags.

TWO VS. ONE

This activity emphasizes throwing and catching on the move, fakes, and defense. To start, you need three players and nearly any type of sport ball.

Two players try to complete five consecutive passes while the middle (defensive) player tries to intercept. Players change places after each miss or five consecutive completions.

Options:
- Pass with your foot.
- Throw ground balls.
- Receiver must be moving.

NOVEMBER

OFFENSE AND DEFENSE

SUNDAY	MONDAY	TUESDAY	WEDNESDAY	THURSDAY	FRIDAY	SATURDAY
PLAY IS NOT WORK WORK IS NOT PLAY	DRIBBLE / FLAG PULL	UP and DOWN	Ask a parent to stand with legs apart 6' away. Can you kick a rolled-up sock through his or her legs? How many times can you kick through in 1 minute?	Face a partner in a push-up position with a tennis ball in between. From the push-up position, try to slap the ball between your partner's hands for a goal. Play a game to 20.	Place an 18" strip of cloth on each hip. Face partners across a field & take turns trying to strip each other's flags as you run to the opposite side.	Practice throwing a ball upward & catching above and below your waist.
Find a balloon. Can you bump it 20 times in a row using only your forearms?	Place a marker (penny) between you & a partner & try to move it by bouncing a ball back and forth.	Practice alternating toe taps on the top of a soccer ball or basketball.	Play a giant game of marbles using 2 tennis balls.	Place an old necktie or strip of cloth in your back pocket & try running passed a partner without losing it.	In groups of 3, throw 3 balls in the air and catch a different one each time.	Race a friend on a series of short backward & sideways sprints. Try not to cross your legs.
Practice dribbling a ball with 2 people guarding you.	Play a shadow game where you chase someone staying just close enough to touch every 3 seconds.	Find a safe sidewalk & practice dribbling a ball without going off the cement.	Face a partner with a ball. Take turns passing the ball back & forth, taking a step back after each successful catch.	Challenge someone to a "Who Can Go the Longest" contest each time a TV commercial comes on. Who can sit with arms & legs raised or stand on one foot the longest?	Practice tossing a small ball upward. Can you catch it above your head? When running AND jumping?	Work on dribbling with your opposite hand & foot.
Find a basketball and goal, & work on setting a new personal record for consecutive baskets.	See if you can match yesterday's basketball record when someone is guarding you.	Find a tennis ball & some stairs. Work on throwing against the stairs and catching the rebound.	Practice throwing & catching with a partner while both of you are moving.	Find someone your own size & an open space. Stand back to back, interlock arms & try to push your opponent backward.	How HIGH can you throw a Frisbee™ or small rubber ball & still catch it?	Place a mark on a wall 24"–30" above your head. How many times can you jump & touch the target in 60 seconds?
In an open space, practice SLIDE steps to your left & right. How fast can you move without crossing your feet?	Use a variety of body parts to keep a balloon off the ground.	Support your body weight on 3 different parts for 5 or more seconds.	Practice throwing a ball off a wall with: opposite side to target, opposite foot forward & elbow leading the ball.	Face a partner 15' away & see how many exchanges the two of you can make with a small ball in 1 minute. 2 minutes.	Organize a family game.	

Calendar calisthenics is a voluntary daily fitness supplement conducted outside of school. As homework is completed, parents put a check in the corner box for the day. Small doses of creative

Name _____

Room _____

 # Extra FUN HomeWork

SUBJECT: Mathematics
SPORT: Football
DIRECTIONS:

The offensive players for the big game were dressed in even-numbered uniforms, while the eleven defensive players wore odd-numbered jerseys. Can you circle the players on each team with the *incorrect* numbers?

Return to your P.E. Teacher

MIND AND MUSCLE

The ideas in this section provide interdisciplinary examples of how subject matter can be linked kinesthetically. This interdisciplinary approach should not be isolated into a single unit but actively integrated into every lesson.

No hassle, no tussle, things go better when you use your mind and muscle.

Contents

COLORS

1 WARM-UP

COLOR TAG. Place the entire class on one endline. Select one student to serve as a caller at midcourt. The caller shouts a color, e.g., blue, and all students wearing blue attempt to run past to the opposite endline without being tagged. Students who are tagged join the original caller at midcourt, making passing more difficult.

2 CONCEPT

The ring colors on an archery target have the following point values.

- Middle ring (gold) = 9 points
- Second ring (red) = 7 points
- Third ring (blue) = 5 points
- Fourth ring (black) = 3 points
- Fifth ring (white) = 1 point

Using crayons or felt pens, draw some large targets and tape them on different walls. Working in groups of 3 to 5 students, throw one ball each at the target from a line 20 feet away. After each throw students rotate to the end of their line. Team members *vocalize* their collective points as they occur. Which team can accumulate 25 points first?

3 CHALLENGE

Designate each of the four walls with the following colors and point values:

- Orange = 4 points
- Green = 3 points
- Red = 2 points
- Yellow = 1 point

When you say "Go," students start running and touching all four walls. Before touching the wall the second time, students must touch the other three. How many points can you score in one minute? What fruits and vegetables match the colors on the walls?

4 CLOSER

COLOR CLEANUP. Cut five pages of four different colors into small pieces and spread them across the floor. Designate an even number of students into each color group. Which group can collect and deposit all of their colors first?

Name _____

Room _____

SPORT TRADING CARDS

Create your own sport trading card. Place a school picture in the square below and fill in the related information.

- **Player name** _____

- **Team** _____

- **Height** _____ • **Weight** _____

- **Position** _____

TRAFFIC CONTROL

WARM-UP

DIAGONAL. Place students in the formation shown. Teams A, B, C, and D do 10 jumping jacks in place. Teams A and B switch places, giving high-fives as they pass. Teams C and D continue doing jumping jacks in place. Teams C and D change places, giving high-fives on the pass while A and B continue jumping jacks.

Variation: Try going from the diagonal formation to four circles on a 10-count and then do 10 jumping jacks in the circle.

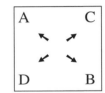

CONCEPT

Set up a circular course. Place students on scooters or the soft side of carpet squares. Instruct students to push themselves around the circle reacting to teacher-held signs.

CHALLENGE

Students find a personal space where (when frozen) they are **not** able to touch another classmate. When you say "Go," students begin walking and changing directions each time they approach someone. When you clap your hands, students **increase their speed** while continuing the no-touch rule. (*Teacher:* Decrease the movement space, challenging good body management.)

CLOSER

FIGURE-8. Mark out a figure-8 shaped running course with cones or other markers. Spread students around the course and have them walk the shape in the same direction. Once students can cross the middle safely, have them begin jogging.

Name _____

Room _____

WRONG NUMBER

Cut out and number two sets of numerals 1–32. One of these squares should have each player's birthdate printed on it. Have a nonparticipant place all of the squares face down in a clear area.

Partners run out (one at a time), pick up a card, and return it to a designated spot. Play continues until the correct date card is located for each team member or ten wrong numbers are collected.

Who can find their date card in the shortest amount of time?

MOVEMENT MATH

WARM-UP

SUBTRACT.   Place students in groups of three or four on one endline. On the opposite end of the floor, place ten objects (beanbag, coins, balls, etc.) for each team. You announce a problem, such as four minus one, and the first person in each line runs, picks up one object, and returns to tag the next runner. As soon as the answer (3) is gathered, that team sits down.

CONCEPT

CONSECUTIVE.   Distribute one jump rope to each student. Explain that *consecutive* means *uninterrupted*. Set a reasonable number of consecutive jumps, e.g., 10. Those students achieving this mark can set their own next goal.

CHALLENGE

Working in 3's (two turners and one jumper), see how many consecutive jumps each student can perform. Have students announce the jump they STOP on as being EVEN or ODD. Next, practice the following skills:

- run through
- jump once in the middle and exit
- jump twice and exit
- jump three times and exit

How far can each group advance?

CLOSER

Arrange students in a large circle holding a thin elastic rope in front. Allow the group 30 seconds to form the following geometric shapes:

- square
- rectangle
- triangle
- semicircle
- diamond

Name _____

Room _____

PREDICTION

How long do you think it will take to do the following activities? Place the estimated time in minutes on the left and the actual time on the right.

- **Walk around the block.**

  estimated time: _____   actual time: _____

- **Jog around the block.**

  estimated time: _____   actual time: _____

- **Make ten baskets.**

  estimated time: _____   actual time: _____

- **Jump rope 100 times.**

  estimated time: _____   actual time: _____

Notorious Bones

WARM-UP

After pointing out 10 important bones in the body, have students find their personal space. When the music begins, students start jogging at a safe speed. Each time the music stops, they FREEZE and point to the bone you call (cranium, clavicle, humerus, sternum, radius/ulna, femur, tibia, metatarsals, etc.).

CONCEPT

SKELETON TAG. Designate 3–5 taggers. Call out a specific target bone, e.g., clavicle. For 60 seconds, taggers attempt to tag as many fleeing students in the shoulder area as possible. Once a person is tagged, he or she freezes on that spot. To become unfrozen, students move their legs apart and raise one hand for help. Other players should attempt to scoot under their legs and "save" as many frozen players as possible.

CHALLENGE

Pass out one balloon per student. Students work on contacting their balloon off the following bones in order: cranium; clavicle; radius; patella; metatarsals. Can they reverse this order?

CLOSER

TARSAL KEEP-IT-UP. Students lie on their back and see how long they can keep their balloon off the floor using only the metatarsals.

Name _____

Room _____

Take Home

COLOR

It has been proven that color can affect performance. For this exercise, you will need a pull-up bar and the following large sheets of paper:

- White
- Black
- Pink (research shows this color has a tendency to reduce weight-lifting proficiency)
- Green

One by one, the sheets are placed directly in front of the person attempting to perform the pull-ups.

Provide adequate resting periods between trials.

MEASUREMENTS

WARM-UP

YARDSTICK. Students place their toes next to the end of a yardstick and practice performing 2-foot jumps forward. How many inches can you jump? Measure from where your last heel lands.

CONCEPT

FEET AND INCHES. In groups of four or five, rotate through the following measure circuit:

- With chalk in hand, face a wall. Reach up as high as you can and make a line. Turn sideways, jump, and touch. Measure the difference—that's your jump and reach. (Use black paper.)
- Sitting on the floor with feet 12–18 inches apart, slide hands forward and see how many inches you can stretch beyond your heels. Keep your knees locked.
- **SPLITS.** From a sitting position with a yardstick across heels, how many inches can you stretch your legs sideways?
- How many feet and inches can you jump *backward?*

CHALLENGE

HIGH FIVES. Partners face at opposite sidewalls. When the music begins, partners attempt to touch as many sidewalls as possible in 60 seconds. Each time partners pass, they give each other a high-five. How many high-fives did you receive?

CLOSER

PREDICTION. How many minutes will it take for our class to jog/walk around the school? Have each student hold up a finger(s) (1–10) representing the minutes they think it will take for the entire group to cover the distance and return to their starting point.

Name _____

Room _____

Take Home

COMPRESSION AND TENSION

In architecture, the formation below is called compression and tension. With six friends you can duplicate this structure. First, stand in a circle (facing inward) with feet together. Intertwine arms as shown and lean back. Where might you see this at a construction site?

COMPRESSION AND TENSION

Source: "Architecture and Children—The Environmental Education Program of the AIA," A. Taylor, G. Viastos, N. Harden, 1987, p. 5. *American Institute of Architects,* 1735 New York Avenue, NW, Washington, D.C. 20006.

LETTERS

WARM-UP

Each letter has a numbered position in the alphabet. Students complete the specified exercise repetition for the following letters:

W = 23rd letter	Do 23 jumping jacks.	
A = 1st letter	Do 1 push-up.	
R = 18th letter	Do 18 zigzag jumps.	
M = 13th letter	Touch 13 walls.	
U = 21st letter	Do 21 hops on one foot.	
P = 16th letter	Do 16 curl-ups and you are done.	

CONCEPT

Here's a way for students to practice dribbling and work on their writing skills at the same time. Distribute one basketball, volleyball, or playground ball to each student. In their personal space, students bounce the ball spelling out the letters of their first name. Once they are able to do this with control, they make large-scale letters by bouncing their name from wall to wall. Switch hands and change directions as necessary. Can you bounce in cursive?

CHALLENGE

Students next exchange their ball for a jump rope. Can you jump out the letters of your first name without missing? Can you jump backward on the first and last letters?

CLOSER

Select two to three class spelling words. Announce the words to be spelled, e.g., whale. Scatter sets of all the letters of the alphabet plus an extra set of vowels at the opposite end of the floor. One by one students in 3–4 lines run down and pick up a letter. If the letter is one from the designated word, the runner brings it back placing it in front of his or her line. If it's not a correct letter, it is placed back (face down) and that runner returns to touch the next player. Which team can spell out the word first?

Name _____

Room _____

ARCHITECTURE

The triangle is the strongest structural form used in architecture. Look at the illustration below and explore some other building models you can copy with your bodies.

IN ORDER

WARM-UP

ALPHA LINE-UP. Place students in four separate lines. In 60 seconds, can they:

- Do FIVE jumping jacks?
- Touch all FOUR walls?
- Do THREE push-ups?
- Line up in alphabetical order (by first name) or line up by height?

CONCEPT

A–B–C. Using the same four groups, place three numbered 2-liter plastic bottles near a wall 20 feet away from each line. One by one, students roll a rubber playground ball at the three pins, attempting to knock them down in *numerical* order. Pins hit out of order must be reset. Which group can knock the pins down in order first?

CHALLENGE

ALPHA BEAM. Tape 2-inch wide strips of masking tape (8 inches long, 4 inches apart) around the room. Organize groups of five at each *beam*. Teams line up first by height and then, without stepping off, discover a way to realign the entire group in alphabetical order by *first name.*

CLOSER

Distribute one rubber playground ball to each group of three. Partner #1 tosses the ball off the wall. Partner #2 catches the rebound and tosses it against the wall for partner #3. Once a ball is tossed, that person quickly runs to the end of the line. Which teams are able to accomplish this in order three times in a row?

Name _____

Room _____

PUT ON THE HAT

For this activity, you will need a hat and a clear area. Place the hat on the floor and discover a way to place it on your head *without using your hands*.

If you were successful with the previous method, try the following:

- *Toss it* onto your head.
- Place it on your foot and *flip it* onto your head.
- Drop it from your head and *catch it* on your foot.

MODES OF TRANSPORTATION

WARM-UP

GET ON BOARD.   Place students in a small circle at midcourt. Designate the four walls as parts of a ship. The front wall is the **bow.** The back is the **stern.** The wall to the right is **starboard** and left is **port.** When you call a location, students run to it as fast as they can. The last two students have to **swim to shore** (lie on stomach and crawl-stroke across the floor on scooters). Once they are safely ashore, they can rejoin the group.

CONCEPT

EXPERIMENTAL PLANES.   Distribute one piece of paper and a hula hoop to each student. Demonstrate two or three folding patterns for paper airplanes. Once students have completed their jets, allow them to throw them toward the hoops (airports) on the floor. How many good landings can they make?

CHALLENGE

BEHIND THE WHEEL.   Students pick up their hoop and pretend they are driving their first new car. Using the hoop as the steering wheel, students move around the room without touching any of the other cars. As students become proficient, reduce the space, creating the challenge of traffic.

CLOSER

A *speeder* is a small car used on railroad tracks. It's powered by two people: one person goes up and the other squats down. Students can create their own speeder by facing a partner and holding hands. Partner #1 squats down and partner #2 maintains an upright position. Alternate and speed it up. They can also try this with a ball between their forearms.

Name _____

Room _____

ABSORPTION

To illustrate how helmets protect riders from head injuries, try the following activity. Find three friends, one large plastic garbage bag, and a small ball. Players hold on to the ends of the bag while the ball is placed in the middle.

The lining of the helmet cushions the impact of a fall. The *soft* tossing of the ball by *flexing* and *relaxing* the bag produces a similar effect. Practice relaxing the bag on impact.

SCIENCE (Machinery)

1 WARM-UP

Spread a number of small objects over the floor. Ask students how vacuum cleaners work. Then time students to see how quickly they can pick up objects and deposit them in a container at midcourt. Report the time and repeat.

2 CONCEPT

The body often acts like a machine. See if the class can guess the following machine actions as students:

- **(Individually)** Create a small home appliance.
- **(Partners)** Create a tool or machine used in the yard
- **(Small Groups)** Invent a large machine with moving parts.

Divide the class in groups and allow them time to demonstrate their inventions.

3 CHALLENGE

CONVEYER BELT.   Arrange students on mats, stomachs down, shoulder to shoulder in a single line. Classmates in the lying position place arms under chest and rock slowly left to right. One by one students at one end begin to log roll on the conveyer belt from one end to the other.

4 CLOSER

Attach three foldable mats with Velcro™ ends together. With three to four students inside, instruct them to crawl forward and backward putting the circular concoction in motion. What machine moves this way?

(**Teacher:** Showing pictures of related machinery provides clearer images of the various machine functions.)

Name _____

Room _____

COLOR RUN

To complete this activity you will need notepaper and a pencil. Your goal, while running around the block, is to find an example of both a primary and secondary color. Primary colors are RED, BLUE, and YELLOW. Secondary colors are PURPLE, GREEN, and ORANGE. See if you can find an object for each of the colors below.

- red: _____
- blue: _____
- yellow: _____
- purple: _____
- green: _____
- orange: _____

ODD AND EVEN

1 WARM-UP

Mark 100 large index cards with odd and even numbers face down in the middle of the floor. Arrange half the students on one sideline (odd team) and the other half on the opposite (even team). Each team places a hoop (for cards) near the middle of each line. On "Go," **_ALL_** players run out and turn ONE card over. If it is an appropriate number, the card is returned to the team hoop. Inappropriate cards are replaced face down. This is a nonstop game. Runners must touch their wall before and after each trip to the middle. Which team can collect all of their cards first?

2 CONCEPT

Make two large foam dice (or use a square box). Opposing teams face 10 feet apart at midcourt. Designate one team as odd and one as even. You roll one die between the lines. If the result is **_odd,_** that team chases the even team back toward its wall. If the result is **_even,_** the even team attempts to tag odd team members. Players tagged become members of the tagging team. For safety sake, place cones ten feet from each wall. Players crossing the cones before being tagged are safe.

3 CHALLENGE

Face a partner. Designate one partner as even and one as odd. Players hold their left hand with palm up and their right hand in a fist. On "Go," players pound their fist in their left hand three times. On the third contact, each partner shows one, two, three, four, or five fingers. If the sum of both partners is odd, that person scores a point and vice versa. Who can score 10 points first?

4 CLOSER

Have the entire class form a single line (shoulder to shoulder) down the middle of the floor. Grab hands and stretch out toward each wall. Does it take an even or odd number of students to touch both walls?

Name _____

Room _____

Take Home

COUCH CALISTHENICS

Try some of the following *muscle-up* activities on your couch and rate yourself using the scale below.

- push-ups with toes on couch (low)
- push-ups with toes on couch (high)
- backward push-ups with heels on couch
- push-up with one leg raised
- push-up with legs far apart
- push-ups with legs crossed

Scale: *Repetitions*
1–3 average
4–10 good
11+ excellent

DECEMBER

MIND AND MUSCLE

SUNDAY	MONDAY	TUESDAY	WEDNESDAY	THURSDAY	FRIDAY	SATURDAY

Critical Thinking

"Being wealthy and wise gets you nowhere if you're not healthy."

Shots / *Hustle*

Take or have someone take your resting pulse. Now exercise until your heart rate increases 50 beats per minute.

How much do you weigh? Subtract your age. Can you perform the difference in curl-ups in 2 minutes?

Lie on your stomach & have someone measure the distance from your head to your toes. How many inches is it? Can you long jump that distance?

Do you think your arm span is equal to your height? Measure three people to see if this is true.

Bounce a balloon off 7 different body parts, starting with your head. Can you name a major bone in each area contacted?

Measure the distance between two telephone poles. How many seconds does it take to run from one to the other?

Write the first three scores for a tennis game.
1 _____
2 _____
3 _____

Predict how many baskets you will make from the foul line (or lane line) in one minute.
Prediction _____
Actual _____

Work on your V-sit & reach flexibility tests. Why is it unsafe to bounce while stretching?

Read your food labels. Find out how many calories you consumed for dessert and do that many Jumping Jacks.

Play catch with a football, then learn how to do your "snap" (number) signals 1–10 in Spanish or French. ("Ready, set, uno, dos.")

Perform 25 push-ups. If someone paid you $1.50 for each one, how much would you make?

Jog and count the number of windows and doors in your house. Develop an emergency exit plan in case of fire.

Predict how many steps it will take to walk one block.
Prediction _____
Actual _____

Practice kicking a soccer ball across a large field. Can you reach the other side faster with long kicks or short quick kicks close to your foot?

Create a Frisbee™ golf course in your yard. Develop a scorecard & challenge your family to a game.

Dance to the oldies & make up a dance riddle. "Like an old game that stretches hands and FEET. A heavy-set singer sets it to a BEAT." (Chubby Checker, "The Twist.")

The average heart beats 100,000 times a day. Take your pulse three times today. Morning _____ Afternoon _____ Evening _____

Work on spinning three different kinds of balls. What provides the spin?

Jog and count the number of windows and doors in your house. Develop an emergency exit plan in case of fire.

Predict how many minutes & seconds it will take to RUN around the block.
Prediction _____
Actual _____

Create a new dance & give it a name that sounds like the actual dance movements.

Practice throwing a ball off a wall at an angle & try to predict where it will rebound.

Count your calories for 1 day. Calories _____ consumed.

Make a New Year's fitness resolution.

Create a 3-person balance where two people are off the floor.

Play a game of sit-up tic-tac-toe with a partner. Find paper & pencil. Alternate sit-ups & mark the grid.

Without looking at a map, write down all of the fifty states you know. Do a push-up for each one you don't know.

Read a sports story in the newspaper. Then go & play that sport.

Print the alphabet while in a push-up position.

Invent a new racquet sport that can be played indoors with a flat hand & a rolled-up sock.

Calendar calisthenics is a voluntary daily fitness supplement conducted outside of school. As homework is completed, parents put a check in the corner box for the day. Small doses of creative exercises can move students toward more consistent exercise patterns. Students will find some mind and muscle activities to provide links between the classroom and gymnasium.

Name _____

Room _____

After running laps in the neighborhood, write
a conditioning rap.

Sample:

"Feel the difference, look the feel. Working out
makes the feeling real."

YOUR IDEA:

Return to your P.E. Teacher

HEART HEALTHY

Heart health activities blend fitness/conditioning tasks with movement concepts on nutrition, stress reduction, substance abuse, and wellness issues.

Exercise early, exercise late, give your body a healthy rebate.

Contents

AEROBIC

1 ## WARM-UP

Aerobic activities make your heart stronger. Examples of aerobic activities are jogging and cycling. A nonaerobic activity is golf. Have students try an aerobic warm-up by pretending to play different sports. When you name the sport, they perform the actions in their personal space.

SPORT	ACTION
• Tennis	Jog in place with forehand, backhand, and overhand strokes.
• Basketball	Jump, shoot, rebound, pivot, pass, dribble in place.
• Boxing	Punch (left and right hands), shuffle forward and backward, jab, undercut.

2 ## CONCEPT

Aerobic exercise is *steady.* Can the entire class jog briskly around the perimeter of the school without stopping?

3 ## CHALLENGE

Place a line of low benches or foldable mats along the middle of the floor. Have partners face from opposite sides, step up and down three times, give each other a high-five, jog to the wall behind them, return, and repeat. How many times can you complete this drill during a 3- to 4-minute music tape?

4 ## CLOSER

EXHALE.   Arrange students in groups of five. Group #1 stands behind a start line, takes a deep breath, and, on the "Go" signal, runs forward yelling "AAAAHHHHH." Each person freezes right where he or she runs out of that initial breath. When all of group #1 are frozen, group #2 takes off. Who can go the farthest on one giant breath?

Name _____

Room _____

STRONGER HEART

Aerobic exercise done three or more times a week for 15–30 minutes can make your heart stronger. Pick out your favorite half-hour television show and see if you can walk in place (brisk pace) from the start to the end of that program. Watch a clock and record the minutes you were able to move in the box below.

Pump It Up

The heart pumps 2½ ounces of blood each beat and 2,000 gallons each day. The average heart beats 40,000,000 times a year! The following exercises will help make your heart stronger.

1 WARM-UP

Arrange students in groups of four and assign one mat per group. Partners #1 and #3 assume a sit-up position (lying on back, knees bent, arms across chest). Partners #2 and #4 hold down the feet of #1 and #3. Following a signal to begin, students perform as many sit-ups as possible in 10 seconds. Next, partners switch places and challenge the scores of their predecessors. Second and third trials are set at 20 and 30 seconds.

2 CONCEPT

Utilizing dynabands or circular bicycle innertubes, students explore different ways to pump up their biceps and triceps. Suggestions:
- Step on one end and curl up.
- Step on one end and pull out to the side.

3 CHALLENGE

With the original group of four, have students lie on stomachs shoulder to shoulder, heads facing the same direction in a push-up position. Number off #1 – #4. When the group is ready, #1 quickly crawls under #'s 2, 3, and 4 and assumes a similar position behind #4. As soon as #1 is in place, #2 crawls under. This process continues until the group moves past a designated line or across the entire floor.

4 CLOSER

- Practice sitting and dribbling a ball.
- Practice lying on your back while dribbling a ball.
- Try doing situps while dribbling a ball. How many situps can you do before I say "STOP"?
- Can you change hands and dribble on the other side of your body while doing situps?

Name _____

Room _____

PUMPING RUBBER

For this activity you need either a 3- to 4-foot strip of surgical tubing or a thin bicycle innertube.

Find a clear space and practice the following:

STANDING

- Step on one end and curl the other.
- Alternate curling arms.
- Stretch across the chest.
- Place under one heel and pull over head.

SITTING

- Place under feet and stretch back, extending legs forward.
- Lift legs and curl and stretch knees.
- Place under seat and pull to the sides.

Things You Can Control

While you can't control your height, the color of your eyes, or when your baby teeth will fall out, there are many things about your body that you can control, such as avoiding lots of sugar and choosing not to smoke.
(*Credit:* Great Activities Newsletter)

WARM-UP

Jumping with a rope continuously allows the body to burn around 500 calories per hour. See how many calories the students can burn in just five minutes.

CONCEPT

CIGARETTE TAG. (**Teacher:** Describe the ill effects of smoking [once you start, it's hard to stop; cancer; bad breath; can't run so fast, etc.] Place one CIGARETTE (student) in the middle of the floor. Following a signal to begin, the cigarette attempts to chase and tag the rest of the class. Each person tagged _chains up_ with the cigarette by placing his or her hands on the person's hips. As soon as four or five students are tagged, it becomes harder and harder for the pack to move. The analogy is that the more you smoke, the slower you run.

CHALLENGE

CHOLESTEROL TAG. Divide students into two groups on opposite ends of the floor. Select two students (CHOLESTEROL) to stand in the middle of the room. Explain that all of the runners are BLOOD trying to get to the HEART (opposite walls) without being tagged by the cholesterol. Each time blood is tagged, it becomes part of the cholesterol. Soon the middle is filled with cholesterol and blood has a difficult time making it to the heart. The analogy is that cholesterol blocks the passage of blood.

CLOSER

CholesterWALL. Have half the class, group #1 (blood vessel walls), form an alley, shoulder to shoulder, 10 feet apart. Group #2 (blood) runs single file through the artery. Each time you shout *"Cholesterol,"* the lines inch closer together, making it more difficult for the blood to pass through. What kinds of things can you do to prevent the buildup of cholesterol?

Name _____

Room _____

Box Out

One of the most exciting events in track and field is the high jump. Find empty cardboard boxes and stack them, one at a time, in a clear grassy area. Practice leaping the first box. Each time you successfully clear the box(es), stack another one on top.

Work on approaching the box from different angles and using a different takeoff foot. When you have missed a box three times, you *box out.*

MINUTE MASTERS

WARM-UP

How many students can master the following 1-minute tasks without stopping?
- Minute 1:   Jog in place.
- Minute 2:   Jumping jacks.
- Minute 3:   Jog in a large circle.
- Minute 4:   Walk at your own pace.

CONCEPT

The heart gets stronger when you exercise regularly. To be able to exercise for longer periods without being overly tired is called endurance. See if students can master each of the 1-minute stations without slowing down.
- Jump rope continuously.
- Dribble a ball while on the move.
- Step up and off a low bench.

CHALLENGE

GOTCHA.   Have students find their personal space. Following a signal to begin, participants move and attempt to slide a beanbag at the feet of classmates. Students struck below the ankle freeze on one foot until tagged (freed) by you. Once a beanbag touches the floor, it may be picked up by any player. How many "Gotcha's" can you collect in two minutes?

CLOSER

EVERYONE'S IT.   In this concluding activity, the object is for students to tag and keep a running count of everyone they touch in three minutes. Have them award themselves a point for each person they tag.

Name _____

Room _____

SHAKE THE SNAKE

Find a partner and a jump rope or six-foot piece of string. Partner #1 holds the _snake_ (jump rope) between his or her index finger and thumb and pulls the slithery strand around the room. Partner #2 attempts to catch the snake by chasing and stepping on the tail. Once the snake is caught, shakers and chasers change places.

Keep It Up

WARM-UP

Distribute one ball (basketball, soccer ball, etc.) to each set of partners. Partner #1 places the ball on partner #2's back. When #1 begins jogging, #2 runs behind holding the ball on his or her back. Switch places every 30 seconds for two to three minutes.

CONCEPT

HIGH-FIVES.   Partners face each other on opposite walls. For the next two to three minutes, they run back and forth from wall to wall giving each other high-fives each time they pass. How many high-fives can they collect? They can walk if they have to, but keep moving!

CHALLENGE

Once again, partners face each other on opposite walls. Partner #1 obtains a jump rope while partner #2 assumes a push-up or sit-up position. A beanbag marker is placed between partners. Following your signal to begin, #1 jumps five times and #2 executes the same number of sit-ups or push-ups. Upon completion, both partners race to pick up the marker. A point is awarded to the person picking up the marker first. Partners change walls and await the next start signal.

CLOSER

Partners lie on their backs with a beanbag between their feet. On the signal "Go," all partners sit up and attempt to pick up their beanbag first. Play the game to ten points.

Name _____

Room _____

Take Home

HEART PARTNERS

For this activity, you need a partner, a watch with a second hand, and a low chair on a nonslip surface (or stairs). First, partner #1 sits on the chair and finds his or her pulse. Once a pulse is found, partner #2 says "GO" and times #1 for 60 seconds.

Fill in #1's resting pulse below.

Now, it's time to exercise. #1 stands before the chair and, following the "GO" signal, steps up and off as many times as possible in 60 seconds. (Partner #2 stands behind and supports the chair.) After the minute of exercise is completed, the pulse is found and the post exercise heart rate is recorded. The same process is repeated by partner #2.

Partner #1
resting rate: _____ (beats per minute)
post exercise: _____ (beats per minute)

Partner #2
resting rate: _____ (beats per minute)
post exercise: _____ (beats per minute)

AT RISK

1 WARM-UP

STOMP OUT THE SMOKE.   While some heart disease cannot be prevented, much of it can. By choosing not to smoke you can add to the *quality* of your life. Tie one end of an 18″ string to a balloon & the other end around each student's ankle. Following a signal to begin, students try to "stomp out the smoke" by stepping on and popping other balloons.

2 CONCEPT

RISK TAG.   Have each student stand in his or her personal space. Place one of the following risk factor signs and a related cause card under each of five softball bases spread across the floor. Next, designate three taggers who will attempt to tag as many classmates as possible. Tagged players must run to the closest base, and pick up and read aloud the cause card before reentering the game.

Bases	*Cause Cards*
• smoking	Daily smokers have a 50% higher chance of heart attacks.
• obesity	Raises blood pressure and harms circulation.
• inactivity	Increases the risk of heart disease and obesity.
• diet	Fatty junk foods are high in sugar and contribute to obesity.
• alcohol	Contributes to levels of fat in the blood.

3 CHALLENGE

For every 75 hours of television viewing, Americans exercise just one hour. During commercial breaks, students should try some of the following for the duration of those ads. (*Teacher:* Demonstrate.)

- From a sitting position, raise arms and legs off the floor.
- Lie on back and bridge up.
- Balance on one foot.
- Work on splits.
- Hold a push-up in the *up* position.

4 CLOSER

24 –7.   Teach students to find their pulse. At this age, most will have a resting heart rate between 70–80 beats per minute. Have them make a fist and squeeze it 75 times in 60 seconds. This is how hard your heart works 24 hours a day, 7 days a week. Exercise keeps it strong. Exercise saves beats.

Name _____

Room _____

BALLOON JUGGLE

For this activity, you need three people and a balloon. The three people grab hands forming a triangle and attempt to keep the balloon off the floor by bouncing it off forearms, heads, knees, and toes. At no time should hands separate. How long can you keep the balloon off the ground?

Options:

- Count the number of consecutive hits.
- Hit off specific body parts.
- Alternate off heads, forearms, knees, and toes.

Relays

WARM-UP

HIGH-FIVE—LOW-FIVE. Establish facing lines of four, 20 yards apart. Following a signal to begin, line leaders on one end sprint to the opposite line, give a high-five to that leader, and move to the end of the line. The student tagged sprints to the opposite line, gives a low-five, and moves to the end of the line. Repeat until everyone has collected five *high-* and five *low-* fives.

CONCEPT

CATCH ME IF YOU CAN. Assign four to six students per team. Set out four different pieces of equipment for each line 10–20 feet apart.

- basketball—10 bounces
- jump rope—10 jumps
- foldable mat—10 steps up and down
- beanbag—10 toss and catches

The first person in line runs to the basketball, performs 10 repetitions, and sprints to the jump rope. As soon as the lead person completes the first task, the second person in line runs to the basketball. The goal is for the person behind to catch up with the person in front. Tagged students continue the circuit.

CHALLENGE

Select partners. Partner #1 sits cross-legged on a carpet sample (slippery side down) or scooter. Partner #2 pulls (with one or two hands) #1 across the floor and #1 pulls #2 back. Which team can complete five trips to the opposite wall and return first? Remember to stay in your lane.

CLOSER

AROUND-THE-BASES RELAY. Place half the class behind second base and the other behind home plate. On the "Go" signal, lead runners run the bases counterclockwise touching all the bases before tagging the next person in line. Which team can complete the rotation first?

Name _____

Room _____

Take Home

RUN THE BLOCK

I WALKED THE TALK
AND RAN THE BLOCK

Date: _____

Name: _____   Completed _____ laps around
the block.

_____

Parent Signature

Nutrition/Exercise

WARM-UP

FRUIT–VEGETABLE. Spread the class evenly up and down one sideline. Provide vests, pinnies, or other colored markers for half the class. Designate that team as the **vegetable group.** The other team represents the **fruit group.** You begin the warm-up by calling either a fruit or vegetable. That group tries to cross the middle without being tagged by one of three taggers. *Tagged* players become additional taggers in the middle.

CONCEPT

FOOD CHAIN. Healthy foods and regular exercise can help keep your weight down, make you stronger, and look and feel better. Have students stand in their personal space with eyes closed. You walk by and whisper one of the following in each person's ear (apple, carrot, banana, broccoli). Following a signal to begin, students place palms up (safety bumpers) and walk slowly forward shouting their particular food choice. As similar choices encounter, they grab hands and rhythmically shout their food attempting to attract all of the other "same foods" to their line. Which group can form their **food chain** first? Remind them to keep their eyes closed.

CHALLENGE

HOT POTATO. Did you know that a potato is a vegetable? Have partners face each other 10 feet apart. Distribute one tennis ball per set. Put on a record or tape of "Pop Goes the Weasel." Partners exchange the ball back and forth quickly (because it is hot). Partners try not to have possession when the "pop" occurs.

CLOSER

APPLE PASS. Have the class form three to four single lines. Give a ball (APPLE) to each line leader. Practice the chant *"A-P-P-L-E PASS THE APPLE BACK."* Following the phrase, the leader tosses the ball back to the second person and the phrase is repeated. After a stationary run through, have the class try it while jogging. Passers move to the end of the line.

Name _____

Room _____

Anaerobic activities can only be carried out for short periods of time. Sports such as <u>gymnastics</u>, <u>track</u> (sprints, high jump, shot put, etc.), and <u>weight training</u> that depend on short bursts of energy are good examples of anaerobic activities.

What are three examples of anaerobic activities you can do around the house?

1. _____

2. _____

3. _____

STRESS REDUCTION

WARM-UP

Physical activity is one of the easiest ways to control stress.
Students lie flat on their backs in personal space. Begin by <u>curling toes downward</u> and hold for five seconds. Next, relax feet for five seconds before repeating one more time. Now, *flex feet upward,* relax, and repeat. Continue this sequence with thighs, buttocks, stomachs, fists, shoulders, etc. Remember to include the five seconds of relaxation between tensions.
(Credit: *Lifetime Physical Fitness and Wellness,* Hoeger & Hoeger, Morton Publishing, Englewood, CO, 1992.

CONCEPT

Mark off a circular walking course around the room. (**Teacher:** Play popular music 3–4 minutes in length.) Have students walk at a brisk pace concentrating on relaxing the arms and upper body. Once the music stops, return to a lying position and concentrate on completing 10–15 deep breaths.

CHALLENGE

Speed things up. Instead of walking, have students jog the circular course. How many laps can you complete in five minutes? If you get tired, you can walk. Try to keep moving.

CLOSER

Students sit in a relaxed position. They close their eyes and focus on 50 slow deep breaths. Breathe **_in_** through the nose and **_out_** through the mouth.

Name _____

Room _____

COOL IT

Cooling down after a vigorous workout is a safe way to end your exercise period. Cooling down properly puts less pressure on your heart.

The cool-down phase is usually as long as the time you spent warming up. After a long game, bike ride, or run, take a:

- short walk
- stretch your large muscles

This practice will prevent some of the soreness that often follows a hard workout.

HOME FIT

This lesson serves to provide heart healthy movement experiences outside of the normal school day. The skills below are taught and practiced in school and repeated at home.

1 WARM-UP

TV TASKS. Students practice the skills illustrated below and perfect them at home as they watch TV. Each time a commercial comes on, students get on the floor and see how long they can hold the different positions. Can you hold them for the length of the commercial?

2 CONCEPT

Rotate through the following activities, spending 60 seconds at each station.

SCHOOL
- Dance to an aerobics videotape.
- Practice handstands.
- Jog from wall to wall 10 times.

HOME
- Dance to songs on the radio.
- Balance on hands with feet on wall.
- Jog in place during a TV news story.

3 CHALLENGE

DASH FOR TRASH. Students go out to the playground and each time they find a piece of trash (not glass), they pick it up and deposit it in a central container. They try the same thing around their yard or neighborhood tonight. Remember to jog when picking up.

4 CLOSER

Students try 3 activities, with & without chalk, while in a push-up position:
- Write the alphabet.
- Play tic-tac-toe.
- Recite the Pledge of Allegiance.

Name _____

Room _____

SAVE THOSE BEATS

Your heart is the strongest muscle you have. Exercise and good eating habits help make the heart's job of supplying blood easier. Exercise actually saves heart beats. Over the next three days begin a running program around your block. Count the number of laps and try to increase the distance run each day.

<u>Laps completed</u>:

Day One _____

Day Two _____

Day Three _____

TOTAL LAPS _____

JANUARY

HEART HEALTHY

SUNDAY	MONDAY	TUESDAY	WEDNESDAY	THURSDAY	FRIDAY	SATURDAY
			I don't have time to exercise. WRONG! You don't have time NOT to exercise.			**M**ake a fitness resolution for the New Year.
Jog up & down the stairs 10 times.	**T**ry to do 25 push-ups with your hands on the edge of your kitchen counter.	**H**ow long does it take to do 100 jumping jacks?	**W**ith the help of a parent, find out the number of fat grams you consumed today.	**T**ake your resting pulse 3 times today. Morning:____ Afternoon:____ Evening:____	**I**nline skate or ride your bike for 20 minutes.	**S**kip a block, gallop a block, jog a block.
Practice stretching each time a commercial comes on TV.	**R**ecord your heart rate before exercise:____ 5 minutes after exercise:____	**F**ind some stairs & work on different (safe) ways to move up & down.	**B**low up a balloon & tap it into every room in the house. Can you do this 5 times in 2 minutes?	**G**rab hands with a partner & see who can touch the other partner's foot 10 times first.	**J**og around the block while raising & lowering soup cans in each hand.	**K**ick a rolling ball while running (jogging) for 5 minutes.
Take a 30-minute walk with your family.	**P**lay a high-speed tag game in a safe place.	**L**ay a broomstick on the floor. How many times can you jump over it in 2 minutes?	**F**ind a partner. Use an empty plastic bottle as a pin & agree on a challenge, like 10 jumping jacks. See who can beat the challenge & knock down the pin first.	**W**ith a real or an imaginary jump rope, jump in place for 3 minutes.	**S**how your family something you learned in P.E.	**B**eat your block run time from last week.
Jog in place for 3 minutes.	**D**ance to 3 fast songs on the radio.	**M**easure off 100 feet. Practice sprinting this distance 10 times.	**W**ho in your family can do the most jumping jacks in 60 seconds?	**G**o cross-country skiing across your floor using towels.	**P**ractice a sport you can play when you become an adult.	**L**ist three foods you consumed today that are heart healthy like orange juice, vegetables, etc.
Find an exercise to do during your favorite TV show.	**S**et a record for running around the block.					

UNEEDPE

ONE ARM PUSH UP

TOWEL RACE

Calendar calisthenics is a voluntary daily fitness supplement conducted outside of school. As homework is completed, parents put a check in the corner box for the day. Small doses of creative exercises can move students toward more consistent exercise patterns. Students will find some mind and muscle activities to provide links between the classroom and gymnasium.

Name _____

Room _____

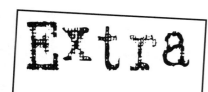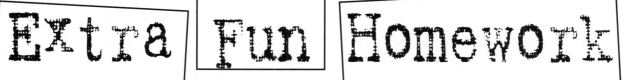

Fitness Promises

I exercise _____ *times a week by doing* _____

_____

_____

When I am in high school I will stay in shape by _____

_____

_____

After school I will continue to exercise by doing _____

_____

_____

Return to your P.E. Teacher

SENDING AND RECEIVING

This section concentrates on utilizing both sides of the body, proper catching and throwing techniques with a variety of apparatus, and locomotor skill combinations that lead to success.

We need to fill a child's bucket of self-esteem so high that the rest of the world can't poke enough holes in it to drain it dry.

Contents

SIDE TO TARGET

1. WARM-UP

Arrange students in open (general) spaces around the room. On "GO," students start jogging. Each time the *freeze* signal is given, see how quickly they can freeze with the <u>throwing hand up</u> and the <u>opposite foot forward</u>.

2. CONCEPT

OPPOSITION. Work here centers on overhand and underhand deliveries. Have students rotate through the following learning centers. *Freeze* students frequently to demonstrate their understanding. Check for side to target and opposition when:

- Throwing Nerf™ footballs through suspended hoops.
- Underhand tossing beanbags into wastepaper baskets.
- Throwing at balloon targets taped to a wall.

3. CHALLENGE

THE TEST. Place six to eight students behind a restraining line some 15–20 feet from a wall. In *slow* motion, check the following movements in the follow-through phase:

- weight on opposite foot
- throwing shoulder forward
- ball hand points at target

Once this pattern is understood, complete a 60-second throwing test (20′ from wall) with the waiting students counting the number of catches. Can you catch your age (6, 7, 8, etc.) in 60 seconds?

4. CLOSER

PINDOWN. Divide the class into two equal teams on opposite sides of the room. Place three empty 2-liter plastic bottles on each endline. Place 20+ beanbags on the center line. Following a signal to begin, the students run to the bags and slide them with good opposition toward their opponents' pins. Students stay on their side.

Name _____

Room _____

PENNY PUSH

For this activity you will need a partner, a penny, crayon or chalk, a large bouncy ball, and a smooth paved area.

Mark a line on the ground and place your penny on the line. Each partner takes two big steps back from the penny and attempts to move it toward one another as he or she executes chest bounce passes.

ON THE MOVE

WARM-UP

HIGH, MIDDLE, LOW. Have students find a personal space and distribute one bean bag per person. Following a signal to begin, students toss their bag high into the air, jump and catch. On the second throw they must toss high, complete a 360 turn and catch at waist level. The third high toss must be caught when the student is on his/her back or, both knees. Each correct catch gets a point. Have students see how many points they can collect in two minutes?

CONCEPT

KEEP-AWAY. Distribute a small rubber playground or tennis ball to each group of three. Players #1 and #2 play catch while #3 tries to intercept. Encourage all players to be on the move.

CHALLENGE

TWO AT ONCE. Students find a partner, obtain two bean bags and face each other six feet apart. They practice moving in a circle (counter-clockwise) and exchanging bags. They can use their own signal to send and receive. Both bags must be tossed at once.

CLOSER

HOT POTATO. Students form a triangle and practice sending and receiving the ball quickly around the perimeter. When you clap your hands, students change the direction of their passes. (*Modification:* This time, after students pass, they complete an exercise, such as jumping jack, jump/turn, floor touch, etc., before the ball returns.)

Name _____

Room _____

Take Home

Sock-It-To-Me

Place a tennis ball inside a long tube sock or nylon stocking. Knot the sock just above the ball. In an open space outside, practice swinging and releasing the ball into the air. As you become more successful, try to release and:

- catch with two hands
- catch with one hand
- catch while on the run
- catch while in the air
- catch while low to the ground
- exchange with a partner

IMPLEMENTS

1 WARM-UP

Pass out one balloon to each student. Following a signal to begin, students try to keep their balloon in the air as they *jog* and bat it off each wall. On the second round, they repeat this task by moving from a crab position.

2 CONCEPT

SHORT STROKES.   Pass out one racquet, paddle, or rolled (and taped) newspaper. Students will use this implement to strike the balloon. From their personal space, students practice short upward strokes maintaining control without moving their feet. Can you stroke the balloon 5 times in a row? 10? Students repeat from their knees.

3 CHALLENGE

Students face a partner over a line. Using the line as a net, they work on keeping their balloon going *back* and *forth* over the line. They alternate striking their object from both the right and left sides of their body (forehand and backhand). How long can you keep it going between you?

4 CLOSER

This time, students try the following between <u>forceful</u> hits:

- touch the floor
- sing a short song
- make a full turn
- do a push-up
- perform a sit-up

Remember, exercises have to be accomplished before the balloon hits the floor.

Name _____

Room _____

SPORT SCOOPS

Cut out an empty (clean) bleach or laundry soap container as shown below. For your ball, roll up a pair of socks. Place the scoop in your nondominant hand and play a game of catch. Practice catching rolled balls as well as balls in the air. How many can you catch in a row?

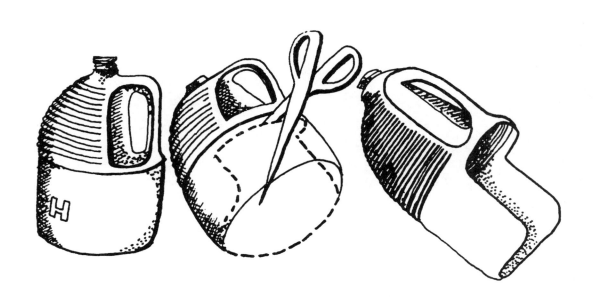

Credit: Elementary Physical Education: More Than Just Games, Bud Turner and Sue Turner. Ginn Press, 1989.

HIT THE TARGET

WARM-UP

HIGH FIVES. On "GO," students begin jogging around the room. Each time they meet someone, they face that person, jump up, slap hands, jog off, and find another target. Repeat for one to two minutes. See how many different people they can high-five.

CONCEPT

PENNY PUSH. Arrange partners on opposite sides of a line 10 feet apart. Place a penny on the line and have students take turns bouncing at the target. They try to move the penny toward their partner. Work can center on specific deliveries, e.g., chest bounce pass, or simply leave the choice to each individual. Stop and replace the penny every 60 seconds.

CHALLENGE

EYE ON THE BALL. Distribute one soccer ball, basketball, or similarly sized playground ball to each student. In open spaces, students concentrate on tossing their ball as high as they can and catching it while feet are stationary. Can you catch it above your head? At waist level? Close to the ground?

CLOSER

HOOP DRAG. Tie a jump rope to a hula hoop. With one partner slowly dragging the hoop along the floor, the other partner attempts to dribble his or her ball inside the moving target. Switch places every 60 seconds.

Name _____

Room _____

Stairs Master

Find a bouncy ball and some high or low stairs. The goal in this game is to toss a ball off the stairs and catch the rebound. Play a game to ten points. Each time a rebound is caught, a point is earned. Missed balls are subtracted from your total.

Options:
- Alternate throws with a partner.
- Catch with each hand.
- Catch before it bounces.
- Return the rebound with a flat hand.

cross dominance

1 WARM-UP

Distribute one tennis ball or small rubber playground ball to each student. In an open space, students place their ball in front of themselves. Following your signal, students begin jogging around the room without touching any of the balls. Each time they hear *freeze,* they stop and balance on the foot you call (right, left, etc.).

2 CONCEPT

Students return to their ball and practice tossing it in a "U" pattern from hand to hand. How many *one-hand* catches can they make in a row? Practice this same skill while bouncing. Next, students stand shoulder to shoulder with a partner. They place their inside hands behind their backs and practice sending and receiving one ball with outside hands.

3 CHALLENGE

Have half the class stand with hands on hips and legs far apart. The other half uses the stationary partner's legs as goals and, in one minute, attempt to hand dribble their basketball, soccer or rubber ball through as many different legs as possible. Trade places every 60 seconds. On the next trial, work on dribbling with each foot.

4 CLOSER

Face a partner from 3 feet away. Partner #1 holds a ball or beanbag in each hand. Partner #2 assumes a hands-up position. One ball is passed at a time (right to right to right/left to left). How many can they catch in a row? How quick can their exchanges be?

Name _____

Room _____

STEP BACK

Find a partner and one small ball. Face your partner. Partner #1 hands the ball to partner #2. Upon receiving the ball, partner #2 takes one step back. Partners continue to step back as long as they catch the ball. Missed balls cause both partners to return to their original spot. How far apart can the two of you get?

Right Back at Ya

WARM-UP

Distribute one small rubber playground ball to each student. Once adequate space is available, students practice tossing their ball upward and catch it before it hits the floor. Can you catch your ball:
- above your head 5 times?
- below your waist 5 times?
- while on your knees (5 times)?
- without moving your feet 5 times?

CONCEPT

Students face a wall and practice throwing and catching balls rebounding off the wall. Students now stand back 15 feet. Can you catch the ball before it bounces?

CHALLENGE

CCC. Students challenge a partner to a 1-minute <u>Collective Catch Contest</u>. Pick a throwing line 15 feet from a wall and see who can collect the most catches in 60 seconds. During the next trial only count the catches students make after the first bounce.

CLOSER

Students assume a sit-up position next to a wall. They lie back, touch the ball to the floor, sit-up toss off the wall, and catch. Repeat, sending the ball fast and slow. How does it return when you throw it forcibly?

Name _____

Room _____

LEARNING TO JUGGLE

Roll up one pair of socks (tight), one for each hand. Practice sending the sock from your dominant hand in a scooping (U shape) motion to the opposite. When the first sock reaches its peak, throw the second across. How many good exchanges can you make without a miss?

SPEED IT UP

1 WARM-UP

Place students in facing lines of three to four 20 feet apart. Provide a different piece of equipment (flying discs, basketballs, soft softballs, etc.) for the first sender in each line. Once the initial throw is executed, that sender runs to the end of the opposite line. After the receiver catches the ball, he or she repeats the process. Play until each line member throws and catches that apparatus; then lines exchange their equipment and a second round begins.

2 CONCEPT

FOLLOW THE BALL.   Set up 4 <u>follow-the-ball</u> stations and rotate each group at 2-minute intervals.

- Shoot a basketball at a goal and catch the rebound before the second bounce.
- Throw a bouncy ball down forcefully and catch the rebound before it hits the ground.
- Stand close to a wall, kick a ball, and trap the rebound before it gets by you.
- Roll a ball at a pin (20 feet away) and retrieve. How many strikes can you bowl in 2 minutes?

3 CHALLENGE

Have partners face in two even lines 20 feet apart. Allow each set to select its choice of equipment to send and receive, e.g., Nerf™ footballs, soccer balls, etc. Following a signal to begin, see how many <u>catches</u> can be accumulated in 60 seconds. Have groups verbalize successful catches "one, two, three."

4 CLOSER

BEAT THE BALL.   Depending upon space, situate a safe number of students on one endline, roll the ball forward, and challenge students to beat the ball to the opposite endline. Speed up the rolls after each rotation.

Name _____

Room _____

Place 10 pennies on a paper plate. Toss the pennies upward and see how many you are able to catch as they descend. Give yourself a point for each penny caught.

Next time, turn over the plate and see how many you can catch on the back side.

Challenge a family member to a sending-and-receiving contest.

Thumbs Up/Thumbs Down

WARM-UP

UP-AND-DOWN TAG.   In this game of everybody's "IT," if students tag someone *below* the waist, that person must do one push-up before returning to action. A player tagged *above* the waist performs a jumping jack before returning. Players cannot be tagged when executing their exercise. This game should have a duration of two to three minutes.

CONCEPT

ABOVE AND BELOW.   Distribute a small rubber playground ball, Nerf™ football, or tennis ball to each set of partners. Players should stand 10–15 feet apart. As partners exchange their equipment, instruct them to catch balls *below* their waist with **thumbs down.** Balls approaching *above* the waist are caught with **thumbs up.**

CHALLENGE

Students practice receiving <u>rolling balls</u> (thumbs down) and <u>fly balls</u> (thumbs up). If the partner throws a rolling ball, return it with a fly ball. How fast can you make these exchanges?

CLOSER

Lying on their back, students play a thumbs-up keep-it-up game with a balloon. How long can you keep your balloon off the ground with hands in a thumbs-up position?

Name _____

Room _____

POPPING CANS

Find a three-pound coffee or syrup can. After you wash it out, place a tennis ball or plastic ball inside. By moving the can up and down quickly, the ball will pop out. See how high you can make it bounce up and still catch it inside. With a partner, try to pop a ball back and forth.

A similar idea is to take a tennis ball and the thin plastic container that holds three tennis balls. Bounce the ball on the ground and see if you can catch it inside the can.

Credit: P.E. Teacher's Skill by Skill Activities Program, Bud Turner and Sue Turner. Parker, 1989.

BODY PARTS

1 WARM-UP

Station #1: Stand one foot from a wall, fall forward, and catch yourself in a *push-up* position. Move a small step back each time you are successful. What body parts are important here?

Station #2: With weight on hands and feet (stomachs up), walk in a crab position across the floor.

Station #3: Practice transferring your weight from hands to feet in an open space.

2 CONCEPT

With a Nerf™ soccerball or vinyl play ball, students practice sending and receiving the ball with different body parts. *CAN YOU:*

- Self toss and tap off fingertips?
- Toss upwards and trap under a foot?
- Dribble from hand to hand? Foot to foot?

3 CHALLENGE

PASS BACK.   Place the entire class in single file. Lying on backs, feet touching shoulders, see how long it takes students to move a large cage or push a ball from one end of the line to the other. All sending and receiving is accomplished with hands and feet as each member gently guides the ball backwards.

4 CLOSER

Place 6–8 hoops or cones in a large circle. Distribute one balloon to each set of partners. Teammates attempt to *alternately* strike the balloon with fingertips as they make their way through the circular hoop or cone pattern. Can you accomplish this without letting the balloon touch the floor?

Name _____

Room _____

HIGH FLYERS

Find a partner and one small bouncy ball. The object of the game is to score 10 points first. Partner #1 tosses the ball high into the air and partner #2 attempts to catch. Catches are scored the following way:

- 1 point for a ball caught (2nd bounce)
- 2 points for balls caught above heads
- 3 points for balls caught in one hand

RULES:

- Partners alternate turns.
- Turns end following a miss.
- Games end when one partner scores 10 points.

Flight

WARM-UP

Stretch a thin elastic rope across the middle of the floor. Two holders (teacher and student) regulate the height according to the task. Place half the class on each endline. Designate one side as Team A and the other as Team B. Calling one side at a time, challenge them to cross:

- jumping as high as possible
- jumping high with hands up
- catching an imaginary ball

CONCEPT

IN THE AIR.   Distribute a bouncy playground ball to each student. Students practice bouncing the ball in their personal space and catching the rebound with hands extended above the head. Can you catch the rebound when you are off the ground? How many jumping catches can you make in a row? Next, students move to an open wall space, bounce the ball before the wall, and catch the rebound.

CHALLENGE

FIVE IN A ROW.   Partners face 10 feet apart. Partner #1 assumes a ready position (knees bent, hands forward). Partner #2 throws five high bounce passes during which #1 tries to catch while airborne with arms extended. Students receive a point for each "good" reception. Alternate.

CLOSER

Have one partner stand while the other is in a sitting position (feet up). The standing teammate gently tosses the ball to his or her partner who taps it back with both feet. How many can you send and receive without the ball touching the ground?

Name _____

Room _____

TARGET PRACTICE

Set up three to four empty and cleaned containers (milk cartons, 2-liter plastic bottles, soup cans, etc.) on a table or box outside. Place the objects in the open or next to a wall but away from windows and other breakable objects.

Using a rubber tennis ball, see how many throws it takes to knock over all of the targets. As you become more accurate, increase your distance from the targets.

FEBRUARY

SENDING AND RECEIVING

SUNDAY	MONDAY	TUESDAY	WEDNESDAY	THURSDAY	FRIDAY	SATURDAY
	ZIG ZAG JUMP OFF	**I**mprove your sending & receiving skills by throwing & catching a ball off some stairs.	**P**ractice juggling. Remember to make a "U" shape as you toss from side to side.	**E**ach high toss you catch in the air is 100 points. 1-bounce catches are 75 points & 2-bounce catches are 50 points. Misses are -100 points.	**W**ork on a handball wall game using your left & right palms as the paddle.	**H**ow many consecutive 1-BOUNCE catches can you make in a row off a wall?
Lying on your back, how many catches can you make in a row with your right hand? Left?	**W**ork on your kicking & trapping skills off a wall.	**B**low up a balloon & create a volleyball game over a modified household net (chair/couch/etc.).	**E**xperiment with throwing a Frisbee™ disc or facsimile. See if you can send it at the right angle allowing you to receive it before it hits the ground.	**P**ractice bouncing a ball forcibly downward & catch the rebound. Can you catch it above your head?	**P**lay a ONE-STEP-BACK game with a parent or friend. Each time you catch, take one step back.	**F**ind two different (safe) objects to juggle.
Roll up a sock in a TIGHT ball & see if you can kick it 3 times in a row using the inside of 1 foot.	**W**ork on kicking for distance. Can you kick farther when punting or kicking from the ground?	**W**hat's the highest height you can throw and still catch?	**U**sing 2 small balls, see how long you can keep BOTH moving with just your feet.	**W**ork on your basketball skills. Shoot & try to catch the rebound before it hits the ground.	**E**xplore different ways to move a ball from your feet to your hands.	**P**lay a "hot potato" game with a partner. Quickly return it to your partner after each catch.
Perfect your cross-over dribble with a bouncy ball. Bounce from hand to hand as fast as you can.	**U**sing a balloon, demonstrate sending & receiving skills from 3 sports.	**P**ractice throwing a ball between your legs & catch behind. How quickly can you throw & still catch? Can you reverse the direction?	**S**tand facing a partner with a balloon between ankles. Can you raise it up to your heads?	**T**ry some wall sit-ups with a ball. Toss from your back, sit up, & catch. How many can you do without a miss?	**F**orm a circle with 3 or more people. How fast can you send an object from person to person?	**P**ractice sending & receiving while ONE of you is moving; while both are moving.
Practice tossing & catching a rolled-up sock while sitting on a chair.	**O**nce again, roll up a sock & play a game of "Rolling Tag." You are "it" if the rolling sock touches your foot.	**S**OCKer! Use Sunday's chair as a goal & practice kicking Monday's sock between the chair legs.		"Most people are about as happy as they make up their minds to be." — *Abraham Lincoln*		RESISTANCE RUN

Calendar calisthenics is a voluntary daily fitness supplement conducted outside of school. As homework is completed, parents put a check in the corner box for the day. Small doses of creative

Name _____

Room _____

Extra Fun Homework

47   That's the number of baskets the average professional basketball player from the "Atlanta Hawks" made in 60 seconds beneath the basket.

SOUND IMPOSSIBLE?

It's not, if you practice each day.

Try this several times and report your best score in the box below.

Remember, you only have 60 seconds!

My best score was:

Return to your P.E. Teacher

ON AND OFF BALANCE

The on- and off-balance lessons in this section focus on integral mechanics necessary for success in a variety of dynamic and static balance situations.

Sports do not build character. They reveal it.
—John Wooden

Contents

STATIC/DYNAMIC

 **WARM-UP**

STATIC: Balance is maintaining a shape while in a stationary position.
DYNAMIC: Balance is keeping an on-balance position while in motion.
Challenge a partner to do the following balance tasks. Who can balance longer on the following body parts?
- one leg
- two hands
- two legs and one hand

Practice raising and lowering yourself in these balances.

 **CONCEPT**

Students find an open space on the floor. Can you move from a balanced position on three body parts to a different position balanced on two body parts? Who can move from feet to hands and back to feet? Can you hop across the floor and balance on the *freeze* signal? (**Teacher:** Share some of the more interesting responses.)

 **CHALLENGE**

BALANCE SQUARE.   Students form a square with different pieces of equipment (thick tug o' war ropes, benches, beams, 2 × 4s, etc.). See how many objects you can cross without falling off. On the second rotation, students change directions each time they reach the halfway point.

 **CLOSER**

HANDSTANDS.   Have mats available. Students practice balancing their weight on hands. What can you do with your legs in this position? Who can handstand their age in seconds? (For example, age 7 = 7 seconds)

Name _____

Room _____

JUMP GEORGE

This activity works well in socks on a carpeted surface. Place a dollar bill on the floor. Stand at one end, <u>hold your toes</u>, and see if you can jump the dollar (lengthwise) without letting go of your toes. Challenge everyone in your family to a contest!

BASE OF SUPPORT

WARM-UP

FACE OFF. Students face a partner two feet away in a catcher's position (squatting, weight on balls of feet). With palms up, can you make your partner move his or her feet by either slapping hands or faking them off balance?

CONCEPT

Students find an open personal space on the floor and practice a balance that is easy to maintain. What makes it easy? *(standing with a wide base of support)*. What can you do to make it more difficult? *(move from two legs to one)*. Have students find three other balances that start wide and end with a narrow base. Is it possible for you to **invert** any of these balances?

CHALLENGE

Encourage students to explore moving in and out of balance. **CAN YOU:**
• Roll narrow into a wide balance?
• Roll sideways to a push-up, lower, and roll again?
• With feet apart, take weight on hands and roll forward? Repeat rolling backward.

CLOSER

PYRAMIDS. Build pyramids with three, six, and ten students. (Add mats as necessary.) What geometric shape appears upon completion? What is the largest pyramid you can construct?

Name _____

Room _____

POWER PICK-UP

For this activity, you need a partner, a clear space, and two small soup cans. Partners face each other (toe to toe) with right hands held. A soup can is placed three feet behind each player. Following a signal to begin, players attempt to pick up their can first. For this to happen, a partner must keep his or her balance while pulling the opponent backward and picking up the can. After a few trials of pulling from the right side of the body, work on pulling and balancing from the left side.

COUNTERBALANCING

 **WARM-UP**

Students find a partner and sit back to back. They interlock arms, push against each other, and see if they can stand up. Are any of you able to accomplish this *without* interlocking arms?

 **CONCEPT**

A counterbalance depends upon both partners distributing weight equally to stabilize their positions. Students create the following counterbalances with a partner where:

- Hands are held, toes are touching, and both are leaning back.
- One partner's hands are supporting the other's feet.
- One person is inverted.
- One partner is standing and the other is at a lower level.
- Both partners are balanced on one foot.

 **CHALLENGE**

Distribute one basketball or soccer ball to each set of partners. Can you balance a ball between:

- backs? When moving?
- hips? When moving?
- heads? From a push-up position?
- feet? When weight is on seats and hands?

 **CLOSER**

How far apart can two partners be to maintain a counterbalance? How close?

Name _____

Room _____

Counterbalancing

Find a partner. The goal of this activity is for both of you to support each other while in an *off*-balance position.

One partner can lend more support than the other. While one balances on one foot, the other may pivot close to the ground with a leg extended upward.

Next, join with another twosome and create a four-person counterbalance.

Weight Bearing

WARM-UP

Students begin skipping around the room. Each time you call *"freeze,"* students assume a balanced position using the number of body parts shown on the card. (**Teacher:** Hold up a card with either a one, two, three, or four.) Showcase some of the more interesting positions. When a card is shown for the second time, challenge students to try a different balance.

CONCEPT

FIVE SECONDS. See if students can maintain the following weight-bearing balances for *five* seconds. *CAN YOU:*
- Step into a balance?
- Fall into a balance?
- Rock into a balance?
- Roll into a balance?
- Jump into a balance?
- Roll out of one balance and into another?

CHALLENGE

How many students can perform the following balance skills?
- Jump from knees to feet.
- Move from feet to hands and back to feet.
- From a lying position on stomach, perform a push-up, clap hands, and catch.

CLOSER

V-SIT. Students assume a sitting position with hands and toes forward. How far can you stretch beyond your toes?

Name _____

Room _____

TV TASKS

As you watch television, you will see commercials advertising different products. These commercials usually last from 15 to 30 seconds. Each time a commercial comes on, see if you can perform one of the balances below. Can you hold a balance for the duration of a single ad? How many can you do?

Credit: Elementary Physical Education: More Than Just Games, Lowell F. "Bud" Turner and Susan Lilliman Turner. Ginn Press, 1989.

Balance Master

WARM-UP

Distribute one beanbag to each student standing in his or her personal space. Challenge class members to balance a beanbag on top of their head while performing the following tasks:
- Turn around.
- Touch the floor with two hands.
- Walk around the room.

At the end of each round, check to see how many were able to keep their bag on top.

CONCEPT

How many of the following balance tasks can students master? **CAN YOU:**
- Stand on a line, perform a straddle jump (legs apart) or pike jump (legs together), and land with both feet back on the line?
- Stand on one foot with eyes closed for five seconds?
- Perform 10 hops on each foot?

CHALLENGE

BEAM MASTER. (**Teacher:** If beams are not available, tape 10-foot strips of 4-inch wide masking tape around the room.) **Can students** walk across the beam:
- forward? backward?
- with a full turn?
- lowering themselves at midbeam and extending one leg?
- lower themselves and touch one knee?
- bounce a ball alongside the beam?

CLOSER

Distribute beanbags to students, who assume a catcher's position with a beanbag on their head. Can you tilt your head and catch the beanbag between your knees? From a standing position, place the bag between ankles. Can you jump, release, and catch the bag behind you?

Name _____

Room _____

Take Home

BALANCE MASTER

To be a "balance master," you must complete the following eight tasks. Check off each one you complete. **Note:** Most of you will not have a beam at home. Place two parallel lines of tape 4 inches apart and 16 inches long on a clear floor.

☐ Lower yourself from a push-up position on one hand and hop in a circle five times on one foot.

☐ Hold one foot, reach down, and pick up a ball.

☐ Hold one foot and touch that knee to the floor.

☐ Hop on one foot and return on the opposite foot.

☐ Balance on one foot, squat down, and extend the other leg forward.

☐ Sit on your seat and raise arms and legs upward for five seconds.

☐ From a squat position, do a Russian dance by kicking one leg out at a time.

☐ Bounce a ball as you walk the beam.

Symmetry/Asymmetry

WARM-UP

Select one student to help hold and stretch a long piece of thin elastic cord or surgical tubing across midcourt. Place half the class at each end wall. Designate one group as Team A and the other as Team B. Ask each group to alternately change sides by running and jumping the rope (1 foot high) without touching it. Can you jump and touch your toes when legs are together? Apart? How high can you be over the middle?

CONCEPT

A *symmetrical* movement is one where both sides of the body are making the same shape. If one side is in a different shape, it is *asymmetrical.* Each movement passes in and out of symmetry. Practice the following movements:

- side rolls
- cartwheels
- jump, land, and roll

Ask students to identify what was symmetrical and what was not.
<u>Place mats where necessary.</u>

CHALLENGE

Select a partner. Make up a **<u>matching</u>** on- and off-balance routine that starts with partners.
1. a. in a side (symmetrical) shape,
   b. perform a matching roll,
   c. and end with a matching asymmetrical balance.
2. d. holding inside hands,
   e. roll away from each other,
   f. and roll back into a matching balance.

CLOSER

Students create two partner bridges that are symmetrical and two more that are asymmetrical. Can you make these bridges open and close?

Name _____

Room _____

CUPSTACK

Find six plastic or paper drink cups and see how fast you can stack them in a 3-2-1 pyramid formation.

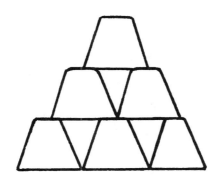

For more information: Cupstack Sports International, P.O. Box 1657, Oceanside, CA 92051.

Acro Balance

WARM-UP

When you call a certain body part, students are to show you how fast they can establish and maintain a balance on that part(s). "Ready?"

- seat
- right arm and right foot
- hands and feet with stomach up
- left foot
- right foot

- head and hands
- toes
- heels
- hands

CONCEPT

This illustration depicts an on- and off-balance stunt that requires the performer to shift his or her weight from side to side. Have students spend a few minutes practicing this move. What other types of weight-shifting activities can you perform? *(cartwheels)*

Leg Circles

CHALLENGE

How many of the stunts below can students perform? *(Use appropriate safety mats.)*

Five-second (L) Lever

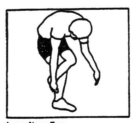

Jump Your Toe

Cossack Kicks or Bear Dance (4 times)

Unassisted Back Bends

CLOSER

DOMINO FALL. Students form a single line with toes touching the edge of a long line of mats. The first person in line falls forward, catching him- or herself in a push-up position. As soon as the first person falls, the second, third, fourth, etc., follow. Students practice until the line falls like dominoes.

Name _____

Room _____

Find a soft carpeted surface and see how many of the following on- and off-balance stunts you can perform.

• Stand facing a wall. Take a step back, fall forward, and catch. Push yourself back to a balance (stand), take a small step backward, and repeat.

• Lie on your stomach, push-up quickly, clap your hands, and catch.

• Find a partner. Face that person with palms together. Practice the first stunt, moving small steps back after each success. How far apart can the two of you get?

Partner Supports

WARM-UP

Working in groups of three, have students discover a way to transport one group member safely across the floor. Can you do this with only **four body parts** touching the floor? Three?

CONCEPT

Students find someone with whom they would like to work. Practice supportive balances while:

- standing (hands to hands, feet to feet, back to back)
- sitting (feet off the ground)
- one partner is off the ground

CHALLENGE

Can you support a partner whose weight is partially taken on *your:*

- hands
- shoulders
- feet
- knees

(**Teacher:** Share some of the more interesting responses.)

CLOSER

Have students stand back to back, bend down, and clasp right hands between legs. Maintaining this position, students alternate swinging legs over one another until they are back to the starting position. Remember, hands must continue to be held.

Name _____

Room _____

DOUBLES

The following partner stunts should be performed in a clear space on a soft surface. Check off the ones you and your partner were able to perform.

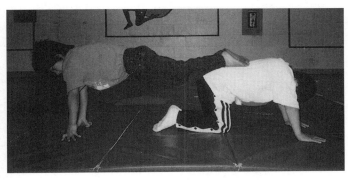

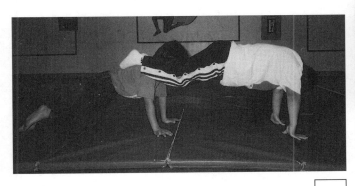

WAND-ERFUL BALANCES

The dowels used in this lesson have a thickness of 1/2 inch to 1 inch and can be found in most hardware stores. The thinness of these particular sticks are not appropriate for combative (wrestling) types of activities.

WARM-UP

JOG AND JUMP. Create an obstacle course (circular formation) by placing wands on top of traffic cones. Students challenge class members to jog and leap each hurdle without moving the wand. After a few laps, ask students to negotiate each new hurdle *differently.*

CONCEPT

Distribute one wand to each student. Ask: In your personal space, **<u>CAN YOU</u>** balance a wand on your:
- shoulder?
- hand?
- toe?
- feet (bottom) while inverted?
- forehead
- Can you move and keep the wand balanced?

CHALLENGE

Students hold their wand with both hands out in front. Can you step over it one leg at a time? Now the wand is behind. Can you step back to your original position without touching the wand with your feet? Is anyone able to jump over the wand without letting go? Are you able to move your legs through when your weight is balanced on your back?

CLOSER

STICK SHOULDER EXCHANGE. With partners facing on all fours, wands are placed on opposite shoulders. The goal is to keep the stick balanced while alternately ducking heads and moving the stick to the other shoulder.

(From: *Children's Games from Around the World* by Glenn Kirschner, W. C. Brown, Dubuque, IA, 1990, p. 131.)

Name _____

Room _____

BALANCING THE BOOKS

Place a pocket-sized book (or similarly sized text) on the floor. With your dominant foot on the book, *try the following:*

- Swing the free leg back and forth and from side to side.
- Extend the free leg forward and lower by bending the supporting leg.
- Remaining in the squat position, execute a full turn using the fingers to support the balance.
- Raise the free leg above the head.
- Hop while maintaining balance.

HIT THE BRAKES

1 WARM-UP

Students find their personal space. When they hear the music, they start jogging. When the music stops, students *freeze* and try to maintain balance without taking an extra step. Repeat 8–10 times, observing techniques students employ to stop efficiently. Allow 10 seconds between stops.

2 CONCEPT

BRAKE CIRCUIT. Teach students how to increase their braking proficiency by practicing the following skills:

- Jump off a springboard or jogger into a hoop (on mats).
- Jump a low hurdle and stop quickly.
- Swing from a rope into a stationary hoop. (Place adequate padding over the swing route.)
- Race a partner from the opposite sidewalls to the middle of the room, back to the sidewalls, and return to the middle. Who can get back first?
- Jump forward in a gunny sack five times and stop quickly.

3 CHALLENGE

Select two to three students to demonstrate actions that help them stop their forward momentum, e.g., bending knees, leaning back, etc. Place a line of mats 20–30 feet away. When you call their birthday month, students run as fast as they can, stopping just before the mat. How close can your toes be to the edge without touching? Students unable to stop can execute a shoulder roll *(safety roll)* onto the mat.

4 CLOSER

SIMON SAYS. Have students find their personal space. Following a signal to begin, play a game of "Simon Says." Mix cues with and without the word "Simon Says." Include jogging, hopping, moving in different directions, etc.

Name _____

Room _____

Take Home

TAI CHI

Tai Chi is an ancient Chinese form of exercise that combines rhythm, balance, and martial arts movements.

- Standing on one leg, practice bending and extending the nonsupporting leg. Move your arms in slow circular patterns.
- Place one foot ahead of the other on the ground. Practice shifting your weight from the back to the lead foot without losing your balance.
- With both hands above your head, lift your right leg. Can you lean forward (with knee bent)? This is called the Crane. Repeat *five* times.
- What animal movements can you mimic in slow motion?

ON AND OFF BALANCE

MARCH

SUNDAY	MONDAY	TUESDAY	WEDNESDAY	THURSDAY	FRIDAY	SATURDAY
ONE-HAND DRIBBLE	**Balance** is the ability to keep an upright posture, while either standing still or moving.	PLAY BALL	**M**ount a bicycle. How long can you balance when the wheels are still?	*From a push-up position, practice bouncing a ball. Every 5 bounces, change support hands.*	**P**lace a small ball between your ankles & jump from room to room.	**H**ow long can you balance on 2 tennis balls? Add a third & see if you can walk across a room.
Walk from room to room while balancing a book on your head.	*Balance on one leg. Place your opposite foot on the inside of your balance leg. How low can you dip in this position?*	**U**sing a piece of tape as your balance beam, practice cartwheels with hands and feet landing on the line.	**C**an you do a one-handed push-up? Try this with each arm.	**H**ow low can you squat on one leg?	**P**lace a broomstick on one toe. How long can you keep it balanced?	**S**et a handstand record (seconds) before you leave for school. Try to beat it when you come home.
Discover 3 ways to roll into a balance.	**H**old on to your toe & see if you can jump over it.	**W**hile balancing on 1 foot, see if you can lower yourself, extending the opposite foot.	**H**old one foot & see if you can pick up a small object on the floor.	**P**ractice balancing during TV commercials. Can you balance for the entire ad?	**O**n what foot can you balance the longest? Right _____ seconds Left _____ seconds	**H**old a broomstick in front of you. Can you step over it and back without losing balance?
Practice the Limbo. How low can you go & maintain your balance?	**C**hallenge a family member to a one-foot balance contest.	*Create a group balance using your entire family.*	**B**alance on one foot. Can you touch the floor with your hands? Opposite knee?	**W**ork on your cartwheels holding the handstand in the middle.	*Sitting on the floor, raise your legs & arms. How long can you hold this balance?*	**P**lace a dollar bill on the floor. Hold both toes & see if you can jump over it without letting go of your toes.
Find a way to balance close to the floor.	*Practice moving up & down some stairs. Try to balance (one leg) on each stair for 5 seconds.*	**W**ith a real or imaginary jump rope, practice jumping to 100 while alternating feet.	**F**ind 2 ways to SAFELY balance a partner.	**B**alance a coin on your foot. Can you hop across the room without dropping the coin?	**P**ractice flipping pennies & catching on the back of your hand.	

Calendar calisthenics is a voluntary daily fitness supplement conducted outside of school. As homework is completed, parents put a check in the corner box for the day. Students will find some mind and muscle activities to provide links between the classroom and gymnasium. Small doses of creative exercises can move students toward more consistent exercise patterns.

Name _____

Room _____

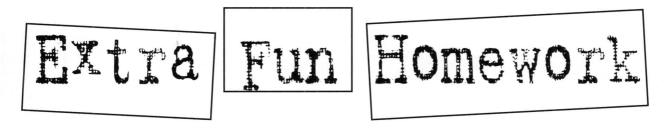

Draw a picture of yourself performing a balance at a *high level* and one showing you balancing at a *low level*.

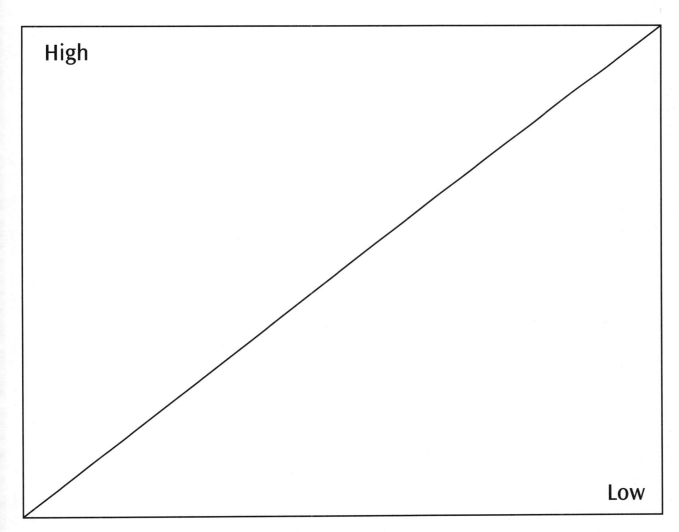

Return to your P.E. Teacher

MUSCLE-UP

Activities in this section focus on camouflaging fitness through a variety of individual, partner, and small group tasks. Becoming fit is hard work. By making them fun, students will work longer and will be more apt to participate at home.

I don't have time to exercise. WRONG. You don't have time NOT to exercise.

Contents

PUMPING RUBBER

For this lesson, students need either one dynaband, a 3-foot strip of surgical tubing, or a thin bicycle innertube.

WARM-UP

Distribute one of the above-mentioned bands to each student. From their personal space, students stretch their band across their chest 10 times, place it on the floor, touch all four walls, return to their band, and repeat this process **three** times.

CONCEPT

CURLS. Students place one end of their band firmly under their right foot and the other end in their right hand. With a **palms-up** grip, students practice curling the band upwards 10 times. Try two sets of ten before switching to their left hand. Next, students assume a sitting position, place the band around both feet, and curl forward 20 times.

CHALLENGE

Students place a band across their feet and hold the other end with both hands. They try to inchworm forward by stretching their feet and sliding their seat toward their heels. How quickly can they accomplish this? Have them race a friend to a designated line.

CLOSER

TASK. Encourage students to discover a different way to use their exercise equipment. For example, like a sling shot (shooting a beanbag against the wall).

Name _____

Room _____

DECATHLON

The decathlon is a two-day Olympic event. Many people think the decathlon determines who is the "World's Greatest Athlete." What events can you perform at home?

Event

Home (your ideas)

_____

_____

_____

_____

_____

Shot-put

_____

_____

_____

_____

_____

_____

Javelin

Long Jump

110-Meter Hurdles

High Jump

Above the Belt

1 WARM-UP

The muscles located above the belt are some of the most widely used muscles in the body. Place students in groups of 4–6 and try this warm-up circuit.
- Squeeze a tennis ball 50 times.
- Arm-wrestle two people in your group.
- Work on handstands against the wall.
- Perform 25 sit-ups while tossing a ball off a wall.
- Try some push-ups when one foot is above your head.

2 CONCEPT

Give students a chance to be the teacher. What other activities can they think of that strengthen the arms?

Group Size	Sample Activity
individual	wall push-ups
partners	pull your partner over a line
trios	three-way tug-o'-war

3 CHALLENGE

Set out enough mats allowing four students per mat. Students find a classmate (close to their size) to be their partner. All of the activities the students just completed used arms. Now they'll work on shoulders. Partners kneel shoulder to shoulder, with arms crossed at the chest. Following a signal to begin, partners attempt to push (with shoulders) their opponent onto his or her side.

4 CLOSER

Students sit facing a partner over a line and hold hands. If they were in a boat, show how they would row. Work those arms. Next, try to pull one partner up to a stand. That partner returns to a sitting position and pulls the other up to a stand.

Name _____

Room _____

Take Home

COUCH CALISTHENICS

Try some of the following muscle-up activities on your couch and rate yourself using the scale below:

- push-ups with toes (low) on couch
- push-ups with toes (high) on couch
- backward push-ups with heels on couch and hands on floor
- push-ups with legs crossed

Scale: 1–3   average
              4–10   good
              11+   excellent

Power Pulls

WARM-UP

This 1- to 2-minute warm-up will determine how fast students can move and increase their pulling power at the same time. When you say "GO," students move from one sidewall to the other in a crawling (stomach-down) position. When they reach the wall, see if they can walk their feet up backwards. When their feet are as high as they can go, students come down slowly and crawl to the opposite wall (with stomach up) and do the same.

CONCEPT

(**Teacher:** Locate an area with enough overhead bars to cover half the class.) Designate half the class as **_runners_** and the other as **_hangers_**. Following a signal to begin, **_hangers_** hang for as long as they can with feet off the ground. When a student's feet touch, he or she sits down. **_Runners_** run around a traffic cone situated 50 feet away; each time they return they give you a high-five. You vocalize each hand slap until the last person on the bars comes down. Switch groups and repeat.

CHALLENGE

TUG-O'-WAR.   Place the same groups in two single facing lines five feet apart. Place a traffic cone 15 feet back from the first person in each line. On "Go," team #1 tries to pull the other team past its team cone. Try this standing and sitting. *(Don't attempt this with a rope thickness of less than one inch.)*

CLOSER

WATER SKIING.   Partner #1 sits on a carpet square (slippery side down). Partner #2 pulls #1 using a short, thick piece of rope. Set up a start and finish line for a water-skiing race. Change partners after each lap.

Name _____

Room _____

DRAWBRIDGE

For this activity you will need a basketball, volleyball, or rubber playground ball. Assume a sitting position and rest your ball on top of both ankles. Slowly raise your feet, drawing the ball toward your thighs. By raising your bottom off the floor, the ball will return to your ankles. How fast can you roll the ball up and down without losing control?

Find a partner. Sit facing with toes touching and pointed toward the floor. Create a track where the ball can travel from one person to the next. Remember to keep your toes pointed.

Repetitions

WARM-UP

REP RACE.   Let's have a repetition race. Line up in groups of three behind one end line. Following a signal to begin, the first person in line runs to the opposite endwall, completes one push-up, and returns slapping the hand of the second person in line. Players who follow add one more push-up per trip. If each student runs three times, the team will accumulate 45 repetitions.

CONCEPT

SLO-MO REPS.   To get the most out of repetitions, students have to do each exercise fully. Try each of these partner activities in slow motion:
- jumping jacks with inside hands held
- alternating curl-ups with toes touching
- partner jump-rope jumps
- standing with knees bent, backs against each other for 30 seconds

CHALLENGE

60-SECOND CIRCUIT.   See how many repetitions students can do with the following exercises in 60 seconds. Record scores after each 1-minute interval.

- jumping jacks

- step-turns off (bench or mat)

- pass a ball off a wall

- sidewall touches

SCORE CARD	
Name _____	
Exercise	**Reps**
Jump Jacks	_____
Steps	_____
Ball Pass	_____
Wall Touches	_____

CLOSER

PARTNER PULL-UPS.   Students select a new partner. Place Partner #1 on his or her back with arms extended upwards. Partner #2 straddles #1 while holding a 1-inch thick dowel. Work on pull-ups with backs straight.

Name _____

Room _____

MUSCLE WORM

Starting from a push-up position, inch your toes forward (knees straight and hips high) walk forward with hands, perform a push-up, and repeat.

Moving this way, how long does it take to touch every door on one floor of your home? How many push-ups did you perform?

LEGS ONLY

1 WARM-UP

Distribute one towel per student. Standing on top of a towel with feet spread, students practice moving their feet in and out to move the towel forward and backward. With feet remaining on the towel, students race across the floor. How long does it take to touch all four walls?

2 CONCEPT

Find a partner and rotate through the following *LEGS* circuit:
- Stand back to back and try to push each other over a line.
- Practice lifting and exchanging a ball with feet only.
- Race your partner from the mid-line to a wall and back.
- Tie a jump rope around inside legs and have a 3-legged race.
- Lie down (facing hip to hip), raise inside legs, hook ankles, and try to pull your partner over.

3 CHALLENGE

60-SECOND STEP TEST.   Facing a stable bench or folded mat, students practice stepping up and down as many times as possible in 60 seconds. Vocalize each repetition. On the second trial, students try turning in the middle and stepping off backward. On the final trial, jump on and off.

4 CLOSER

DOWN THE LINE.   Students sit side by side in groups of four to six with feet facing a wall. Start a ball at one end and see if each player can trap it with feet (on the wall) and move it down the line.

Name _____

Room _____

SOUP-CAN RUN

Many joggers now use 2-lb. hand weights when they jog. Jogging doesn't make the arms stronger, so by adding these weights the runner is exercising additional body parts.

Find two cans of soup. Put one in each hand and jog around the block. Practice boxer-like punches or simply raise them up, down, out, and in as you run.

How did your arms feel following the run?

Resistance

WARM-UP

ISOTONIC.   Isotonic resistance works muscle by using heavy weights or pressure from your own body. Have students begin jogging around the room. When you say "freeze," they move to the closest wall, take one big step back, and place hands on wall slowly lowering themselves toward the wall on your countdown of **"10–9–8–7–6–5–4–3–2–1."** On "1," students' nose should almost be touching the wall. Repeat.

CONCEPT

GIVE AND TAKE.   In these activities, resistance is adjusted to force. Try the following *partner resistance* activities:

- Face each other with palms together. Take a step back and push against each other to maintain balance.
- With toes touching, grab hands, lean back, and hold that position.
- With partner #1 lying on his or her back (arms up), #2 does a push-up on top.

CHALLENGE

VARIABLE RESISTANCE.   Students stand facing a partner with arms extended. Partner #1 places hands outside forearms of #2, and practices pushing in and out. Next, partner #1 lies on his or her stomach with legs curled forward. Partner #2 places one arm across #1's ankles and pushes down while #1 pushes out. Finally, have partner #1 sit with legs apart and #2 with legs inside #1's. Partner #1 presses legs inward and #2 outward.

CLOSER

You increase resistance by adding weight. A good way to illustrate this is by having students do incline push-ups. Try doing 3 with feet two feet off the floor; 3 with feet one foot off the floor; and 3 with feet flat on the the floor. Which were the most difficult?

Name _____

Room _____

TOWEL PULL

Find a partner and one large bath towel. Select a clear, safe place indoors or a grassy area outdoors. Face each other over a marked line. On "GO," see who can pull the other over the line.

Options:

- Try to pull your partner over when you are back to back.
- Try to pull each other off balance from a sitting position.
- While pulling, see who can keep their feet from moving longer.

TIRED OUT

WARM-UP

Muscular endurance is being able to work a muscle for long periods. See how long students can hold themselves UP on the following activities:

- Hold your chin above a bar.
- Hang from a rope(s) without using your feet.
- Maintain a wall handstand.
- Hold a push-up position.

CONCEPT

BRIDGE. Arrange students in groups of six, shoulder to shoulder, in a push-up position. On "GO," the first person in line crawls under the entire bridge. Once at the end, that player assumes a push-up position next to the last person and yells "GO." This process continues until all members have passed under the tunnel. Lines able to accomplish this feat can join with another team to attempt to perform a double bridge.

CHALLENGE

TIRED OUT. Place students inside large truck innertubes over a square section of mats (minimum of 6 mats). (**Teacher:** Duct tape the valves down to protect the player.) Following a signal to begin, students try to bump the other students out of the square. Once a student's foot touches outside the mats, he or she is out. The round ends when only one student remains.

CLOSER

PARTNER PUSH-UPS. Students face a partner 3 feet apart with palms pointed up. They lean forward and catch each other in a push-up position. Gently push each other back to a standing position. Each time they can successfully catch each other, they take another small step back. How far can they go?

Name _____

Room _____

KING and QUEEN OF CARDS

All you need for this activity is a partner and a deck of cards. Remember the game of "War"? Partners alternate drawing cards. The high card takes the low card and the player with more cards wins.

In the *muscle-up* version, partners pick an exercise. The low-card recipient gets to perform the chosen activity (jumping jacks, sit-ups, push-ups, jump rope, etc.). The winner is the person completing more repetitions.

EXPLODE!

1 WARM-UP

Divide the class at opposite endlines. Designate one group as team #1 and the other as team #2. Stretch an elastic stretch cord (1/8-inch thickness) from sidewall to sidewall at midcourt. Choose one student to hold the other end. Call one team at a time to jump the rope without touching. Once a group crosses, it remains on that side until the other team completes its challenge.

TASKS (1 rope 1 foot high)
- Cross jumping off one foot; two feet
- Cross jumping with legs apart; legs together
- Cross making a half turn
- Cross exploding as high as possible over the middle

2 CONCEPT

Students find a line and place both feet behind it. They practice bending knees, throwing hands back and then quickly forward as they jump. Next, try jumping backwards. In which direction were they able to jump farther? Students find a partner. Have partner #1 lie down. Partner #2 marks a chalk line near the top of #1's head and a line even with the heels. Can they jump over both marks? Alternate.

3 CHALLENGE

PARTNER HOOP JUMP. Distribute one hoop to each set of partners. Partner #1 holds the hoop horizontal 1 foot off the ground. Partner #2 attempts to jump inside and back out without touching. Raise the hoop height 6 inches after each success. Switch places after a miss.

4 CLOSER

Students try these explosive movements:
- From a position on your knees, swing arms forward and jump to your feet.
- Lie on stomach, do a push-up, clap hands, and catch yourself.
- Jump and click both heels together.
- Jump and touch both toes.

Name _____

Room _____

Take Home

TIRE THROW

Find an old car tire (or innertube) and a clear open space. Grab the tire with your throwing hand and fling it as far as you can. Next, establish a scratch line. See if you can perform your throws without crossing over the line.

Try throwing from:
• the opposite hand
• a running start
• a circular rotation (discus)

My best throw was _____ feet.

ISO ISO ISO

1

WARM-UP

ISOMETRIC.   Students find a stable wall. Can you pretend to:
- lift it up?
- push it down?
- pull it to the ground?

2

CONCEPT

Try each of these muscle-building activities.
Isotonic: Weight is moved through a range of motion.
- **Mat Carry Relay.** In groups of 5–6 place one person in the middle with the other members on the outside. One by one, each team member is lifted and transported across the room (no higher than one foot off the floor).
- Load backpacks with books and do step aerobics on a bench.

Isometric: Force applied against a stationary object.
- Stand with back against a wall, squat down, and push hard.

Isokinetic: A cooperative activity where force and resistance are balanced.
- **Peace Wrestle.** With partners, experiment with an arm-wrestling contest where both partners attempt to keep arms near the starting point.
- **Stand Up.** Sit back to back, interlock arms, push against each other, and try to stand up.

3

CHALLENGE

PARTNER PULL OVER.   Students face their partner on a line and grab hands. Following a signal to begin, see if they can pull their partner over the line. Play a "best of five" series.

4

CLOSER

List some of the exercises described above and have students identify if it was isotonic, isometric, or isokinetic. Next, have partners create and demonstrate a muscle-development activity and categorize it.

Name _____

Room _____

WALL BALL CURL-UPS

As you get older, the thrill of completing curl-ups may diminish quickly. One variation that makes this activity more enjoyable is by adding a ball!

Sit facing a wall with knees bent, shoulder blades touching the floor, and a ball held behind your head. As you lift your shoulders, throw the ball off the wall and catch it as your torso reaches the upright position.

How many can you perform in 60 seconds?

Junkyard Gym

1 WARM-UP

Utilizing dynabands, 2-foot strips of surgical tubing, or thin bicycle innertubes, complete the following stretches:

Position	*Activity*	*Repetitions*
• standing	• stretch in front and behind	• 25 times
• standing	• step on one end and curl up	• 25 times
• sitting	• sit on top and pull over back	• 15 times
• sitting	• with legs elevated, place around both feet and pull back	• 25 times

What other different stretches can the students perform?

2 CONCEPT

JUNKYARD CIRCUIT

- Step on and off a bench 25 times while holding two sand-filled bleach bottles.
- Fasten a rope to a wall. Sit on a carpet sample (slippery side down) and pull yourself into the wall.
- Tie tubing to the bottom of a chair and press it upwards.
- Sit on a chair and curl two 1-lb. 3-oz. soup or vegetable cans 25 times.
- Place hands inside roller skates and perform some rolling push-ups (on knees and a mat).
- Loop two bicycle innertubes together. Place one tightly in a door and the other around your waist. Jog slowly away from the door.
- Do 25 jumps with a garden hose (jump rope) filled with sand.

3 CHALLENGE

TRASH RUN.   Divide the class into four even teams. Distribute one trash can per group. See which team can collect the most trash in **three** minutes. Remind students to find an adult if coming upon dangerous items such as, broken bottles, needles, etc.

4 CLOSER

Each student finds three chairs. They place heels on one chair and right and left arms in the middle of the other two. How many dips can you perform by lowering your body between the chairs?

Name _____

Room _____

PUSH-UP HOCKEY

Have four people form a square in a push-up position. Each player faces the middle two to three feet apart.

Next, place a small ball or beanbag in the middle. One player will say "GO" and the ball is slapped toward one of the three goals (hands). The ball may only be moved with a flat hand. Goals must go through the <u>front</u> door of the goal, not the side (no catching allowed.) Once a goal is scored, the ball is placed back in the middle and play begins once more.

OPTIONS:
- See how many goals you can score in a specified amount of time.
- Who can score five goals first?
- Who is able to remain in the UP position for one minute?

APRIL

MUSCLE UP

SUNDAY	MONDAY	TUESDAY	WEDNESDAY	THURSDAY	FRIDAY	SATURDAY
Arm Wrestling		The best angle to approach anything is the "Try-Angle."	TOWEL RACE	"We need to get the message out, loud and clear, that quality physical education for every child is a necessity–not a luxury." –Tom McMillen		Squeeze a tennis ball 100 times with each hand.
Find a line on the floor. With elbows at your side, palms up, try to push a partner over the line.	How far apart can your arms be while performing a push-up?	Using some stairs in or around your house, work on moving up, down, & sideways on your tiptoes.	The end of ski season is near. Work on your legs: squat, keep back straight, and hold for 60 seconds.	Lying on your back, place your hands under the couch & press slowly upward.	Find an open field and for 5 minutes practice kicking a ball for distance.	Locate a waist-high object & stretch your leg on top for 60 seconds. Try this with each leg.
Find a safe wall space & practice your handstands. Can you do a push-up from this position?	Sitting on the floor, stretch your legs up a wall. Next, lift your seat & hold this position as long as possible.	Hold a bath towel behind you and stretch it for 10 seconds. Try this under both feet.	Hop around the house on one foot. Jump around it on two feet. How many jumps does it take?	How many bent-knee sit-ups can you do in 60 seconds?	While you watch TV or listen to the radio, do jumping jacks each time a commercial comes on.	Sit back to back with a family member or friend. Interlock arms & see if you can both stand up.
Partners sit facing with feet together. With weight supported on hands, lift legs & seats off the floor at the same time.	Jog your age on each stair in your home.	Face a partner in a sitting position. Grab hands & see if you can pull each other up to a stand.	Jog through every room in your house with a soup can in each hand. Pump them up & down like weights.	Do a standing push-up while facing a wall. Take a small step back after each one.	Set up a family arm-wrestling tournament. How did you do?	Sit facing a partner. Have one place legs inside the other's. One squeezes IN, the other OUT; then switch.
Try a one-arm push-up.	From a standing position, measure in *inches* how high you can jump; how far forward & backward.	Practice jogging up a small hill or stairs 10 times.	Practice some chair back push-ups.	Moving legs in & out have a towel race on a slippery floor.	Sit facing a partner in a sit-up position. Place a ball between you. On "GO," sit up & see who can pick up the ball first.	Try some partner pull-ups. PARTNER PULL
Can you do 10 chair dips?						

Calendar calisthenics is a voluntary daily fitness supplement conducted outside of school. As homework is completed, parents put a check in the corner box for the day. Small doses of creative exercises can move students toward more consistent exercise patterns. Students will find some mind and muscle activities to provide links between the classroom and gymnasium.

Name _____

Room _____

A. Draw a line connecting the muscle to its location on the body.

B. When a star appears, list a sport skill in which this muscle plays an important role.

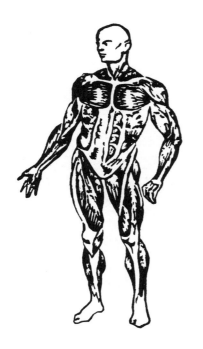

Muscles

Biceps

Quadriceps

Deltoid*

Triceps

Abductors

*Why are deltoids important in sports? _____

_____

Return to your P.E. Teacher

STRIKING

The tennis player in the middle of a serve or a soccer player kicking a goal must be able to display the correct movement techniques to produce desired results. Emphasis here is placed on striking with and without apparatus.

Success is not measured by what you do, compared to someone else. Success is what you do, compared to what you are capable of doing.
—Zig Zigler

Contents

HAND PADDLES

As children become more proficient they will be capable of hitting rebounds coming off a wall. In the beginning, you may want to allow students to drop, hit, and catch the rebound. The majority of the contacts generally take place within 10 feet from the wall. The younger the child, the larger the ball.

WARM-UP

Students find an open wall. They place their dominant hand (hand you throw with) against the wall. Give the wall a high-five; low-five. These are basic handball strokes. Next, students place both hands on the wall, back up, and practice push-ups.

CONCEPT

Distribute one 6- to 8-inch rubber playground ball or high-density Nerf™ tennis ball to each student. Students find a clear wall space and practice dropping the ball and striking it off the wall with an open (tight) hand. Encourage students to use both their dominant and nondominant hands to strike the ball. Have students think about how old they are. During the next five minutes, see if they can contact the ball before the second bounce as many times as they are old; e.g., age 7 = 7 consecutive contacts. How many of them surpassed their age in hits?

CHALLENGE

How many of you can *return* the ball when:
• it's over your head?
• it's low to the ground?
• it's on your nondominant side?
How many rebounds can students strike in a row?

CLOSER

ALTERNATING HITS. Have students play a game with a partner. Partner #1 starts by dropping and striking the ball while #2 plays the rebound. Partners score a point each time they can alternate hits successfully. Remember, you can't hit the ball twice in a row.

Name _____

Room _____

KICK-OFF CAN

Practice kicking for distance. Find a clear space outside. Balance a playground ball, football, or soccer ball on the open end of a cleaned soup can. Practice different approaches contacting the ball just below center.

Level-Swing Plane

WARM-UP

Distribute one paddle or racquet and a perforated plastic or tennis ball to each student. Have students shake hands with the paddle and balance the ball in the middle. On "GO," students start walking slowly around the room. If they can keep the ball balanced moving slowly, they can try to keep balanced while jogging. Remind students to watch where they're going.

CONCEPT

Some say that half the game of tennis is just picking up the ball! Let's see how long students can avoid picking up their ball by hitting it softly off the wall using the middle of the paddle and a consistent level swing. Try these important tips:
- side to target
- stiff wrist
- paddle back
- step toward the target
- contact the ball over front foot

CHALLENGE

Students select a partner. Standing 10–15 feet back from a wall, students see how many times they can alternately contact the ball in one minute. Each time a miss occurs, students should quickly pick it up, return to the line, and continue striking until they hear the signal to stop.

CLOSER

In groups of four, see how many balls students can pick up and transport (with paddles only) from one container to another. Remember, they can't use hands to pick up or support the balls when moving.

Name _____

Room _____

FOOT GOLF

(Let's play a game of "Foot Golf." First, find a *soft* ball. Next, mark off nine numbered floor-level targets (with masking tape) around the house. If your home has two levels, keep all of the targets on one level. When the targets (holes) are established, see how many foot pushes (putts) it takes to touch each of the targets.

Holes:

#1 ___ #2 ___ #3 ___ #4 ___ #5 ___

#6 ___ #7 ___ #8 ___ #9 ___

Total: ___

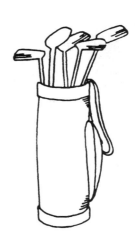

Get Into the Swing

1 WARM-UP

Have each class member find his or her own *personal* space. After covering the batting tips below, have students grip an imaginary bat, swing, and sprint through a clear pathway. Repeat. Be aware of the other batter's running patterns.

Batting tips:
- eye on the ball
- quick level swing
- don't throw the bat
- cover the plate

2 CONCEPT

CONE BALL BASICS. Spread traffic cones (18 inches high or above) in a single line 20 feet apart. Place one plastic bat and perforated ball by each cone. Organize groups of students safely (minimum 15 feet) behind each cone. One by one, students approach the cone and, on the signal "SWING," practice hitting the ball off the cone. Once all balls are hit, players pick up their ball, replace it on the cone, give the bat to the next batter, and return to the end of the line.

3 CHALLENGE

Assign teams of three batters and three fielders to each cone. Place a second cone 20–30 feet from the *home* cone. The batter's challenge is to hit the ball and beat it to the second cone. If the runner is tagged on the way or the cone is touched with the ball first, the batter is out. Runners who are safe must run home on the next batted ball. Allow three outs before changing sides.

4 CLOSER

Run a long rope or thin elastic cord down the middle of the floor. Suspend perforated plastic balls to the line 10–15 feet apart. Give each student three swings. Hit balls that swing above the rope are hits. Balls making a full circle are homeruns.

Name _____

Room _____

HOMEBOWL

Clean out three 2-liter plastic containers or milk cartons and stack them in a 1–2–3 formation 2–3 inches apart. Using a *soft* ball, practice rolling it at the pins from a distance of 10 or more feet. Take ten rolls, replacing fallen containers after each turn. Score the number of pins knocked over after each roll.

#1 ____   #6 ____

#2 ____   #7 ____

#3 ____   #8 ____

#4 ____   #9 ____

#5 ____   #10 ____

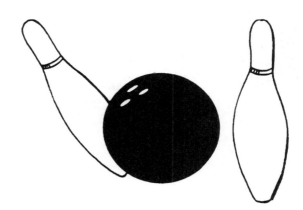

After a few rounds, challenge a family member to a game.

HIT PARADE

1 WARM-UP

BALLOON TAG.   Distribute one 9- to 11-inch balloon to each student. Following the signal to begin, students start walking (a quick walk is allowed) and striking their balloons upward. Players must continue tapping their balloons while attempting to tag other players. Tags only count while balloons are in the air.

Variations:
* Exchange balloons following a tag.
* Use a limited number of colors so students can try to tag another player in each color group.

2 CONCEPT

HIT PARADE.   Have students work on the following parade of hits. Can you strike your balloon **three times in a row** off your:

* <u>hairline?</u>   (soccer)
* <u>instep?</u>   (soccer; football)
* <u>forearms?</u>   (volleyball)
* <u>flat palm?</u>   (racquet sports)
* <u>wrist?</u>   (volleyball)
* <u>fingertips?</u>   (volleyball)

3 CHALLENGE

FOUR-WALL TAP.   Students select partners. How quickly can partners alternately strike *one* balloon off all four walls and return to their starting spot?

4 CLOSER

TRAP AND TAP.   Arrange students in single lines of six to ten, lying on backs (feet touching shoulders of the person ahead, hands up). Following a signal to begin, the first-person line gently taps the balloon from the front to the back of the line. Each person must trap and tap on the way. Which group can trap and tap its balloon from the front to the end and back home first?

Name _____

Room _____

Shoebox Derby

Find some old shoeboxes and a carpeted surface—and get ready to skate across the floor. With a foot in each box, practice skating by sliding your feet in and out (shape of a "V"). As you become more proficient, put a ball between the boxes and practice pushing it back and forth between your feet.

How quickly can you move the ball around the room?

Delivery Speed

The faster the implement or body part is moving on contact, the more power is generated. This lesson will focus on controlling a ball with both full and short swings.

 **WARM-UP**

Students find an open space outside where their swing will not interfere with others. When you call the month in which they were born, students come and find a paddle/racquet and ball. On your signal, they practice hitting the ball as far as they can, place the racquet on the ground, retrieve the ball, and await the next signal to hit.

CONCEPT

Find a clear wall space (inside or out). Students practice striking the ball off their paddle when the *swing-side elbow* is *in* and when it is *extended*. (**Teacher:** Demonstrate this concept.)

CHALLENGE

Students face the wall 10–15 feet back and work on ten soft (short-swing) strokes followed by ten hard (full-swing) strokes. What gives you more power? Accuracy? How many can you hit in a row?

  **CLOSER**

Students find a partner and see if they can alternate hits off the wall. Allow only one bounce between hits. Which team can record the most hits in a row?

Name _____

Room _____

JUMPING-JACK SOCCER

For this activity, you will need one or more friends, a clear space, and one tennis ball. Player(s) without the ball stand with legs apart. The player with the ball uses feet to move the ball through the open legs as quickly as possible.

After trading places, have the standing player(s) perform <u>jumping jacks</u>, making the shots on goal more difficult for the dribbler.

Set up an obstacle course and time each player as they dribble through.

KEEP IT UP

WARM-UP

Distribute one volleyball-size balloon to partners facing on opposite sides of a line. They must work together to keep the balloon going without moving their feet. See if students can perform a jumping jack, a push-up, etc, between hits.

CONCEPT

Call out specific bones (e.g., cranium, femur, metatarsals) and muscles (e.g., quads, etc.) for students to contact the balloon off of.

CHALLENGE

Arrange students in groups of four lying (feet toward center) on mats. Distribute one balloon per person. Following a signal to begin, teams work on keeping their group of balloons up off the ground using feet only. Once a balloon touches the floor, attention turns to the remaining floating targets.

CLOSER

Place two players on each side of a foldable mat (standing) and work on playing one balloon back and forth. The receiving partner taps the balloon up and his or her teammate spikes the balloon over the makeshift net.

Name _____

Room _____

Grocery Bag Dribble

Find a paper grocery bag and one bouncy ball. Place the bag over your head and see if you can keep the ball bouncing without watching it. Next, dribble a few steps forward and backward. Were you able to maintain control? Can you maintain control using the opposite hand?

Arms Extended

WARM-UP

ExtendedCISE. Find a partner and try these (extend your arms) stunts.
- <u>Standing</u>, place toes together, grab hands, and lean back as far as you can without losing your balance.
- <u>Sitting</u>, with toes together and legs apart, grab hands. As one partner leans back, the other pulls forward trying to touch his or her chest to the floor. Alternate.
- <u>Standing</u> and facing over a line, grab hands and try to pull each other over to your side.
- <u>Jump up</u> to give your partner ten (extended arm) high-fives.

CONCEPT

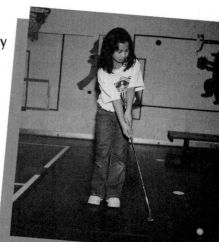

Encourage students to experiment with a variety of implements and swings during the following "Extend Your Arms" circuit. (TIPS: From a ready position, use a firm grip, keep your eye on the ball, extend your arms, contact the ball with a smooth follow-through.)
- Control a ball off the wall with a tennis racquet or paddle.
- Strike a beachball straight up five times in a row.
- Bat a soft ball off a batting-T into a standing foldable mat.
- Putt a plastic golf ball into a dust pan.
- Jump and spike a volleyball or Nerf™ ball held by a teammate on a chair.

CHALLENGE

In groups of three (batter–pitcher–fielder), students take turns DROPPING and STRIKING a small 6-inch bouncy playground ball with a flat extended hand. Who can hit the ball the farthest? Compare the power and distance of an extended arm swing to a ball hit with the hitting elbow held in.

CLOSER

Students assume a push-up position. With feet stationary, they walk their hands forward. How far extended can you be and still perform a push-up?

Name _____

Room _____

SOCK-R-CISE

This exercise uses a tightly rolled-up sock to improve eye–foot coordination. First, stand with knees slightly bent. Place the sock in your dominant hand. Lift the striking foot with the heel pointed toward the opposite knee. The flat surface here is the striking target.

<u>CAN YOU</u>:

- strike two in a row? three?
- strike a partner-tossed sock off this same target?
- drop and return the sock to a partner?

"Popping Can" Basics

WARM-UP

FOOT TAG.   Designate two to four taggers with a pinnie or vest. Have students find their personal space. Every time you beat the drum, students may take one giant step away from the taggers. If the drum beats quickly, they can move quickly. Students tagged do five jumping jacks and return following the next beat of the drum. (*Reminder:* Taggers also move only to the beat of the drum.)

CONCEPT

(**Teacher:** *Two-gallon cans are usually available from school lunchrooms. Clean cans are excellent tools for improving striking proficiency.*)
Distribute one tennis ball and can to each student. In their personal space, see if they can:

- bounce the ball three times in a row on the inside; outside
- bounce low; over their head
- alternate bounces off the can and the floor
- bounce off a wall
- alternate bounces inside and outside of the can

CHALLENGE

Students select partners and face each other 10 feet apart. They practice exchanging balls using both the inside and bottom of the cans. How many can you exchange in a row? How far apart can you be?

CLOSER

What kind of *music* can students make with the cans and balls? Get into groups of three and experiment with some new popping sounds.

Name _____

Room _____

 DROP AND HIT

To complete this activity, you need a large open space, one bouncy 6-inch (or larger) playground ball, and a friend. Take turns bouncing the ball in front, extending the striking arm, and hitting it with a fist or open hand.

Practice hitting the ball:
• on top
• in the middle
• below the middle

Where did you contact the ball to make it bounce quickly?

Where did you contact the ball to lift it into the air?

TOUCH

This lesson is best suited for outdoor play.

1 WARM-UP

Assign balls to ten students. Following a signal to begin, players with a ball attempt to dribble it with their feet while remaining students try to steal one away. If they lose a ball, they try to regain it from a different player. No physical contact is allowed—only fast feet!

2 CONCEPT

Distribute one rubber playground ball or soccer ball to each student. Explain that accuracy is determined by the force, angle, or contact point of the kick. Pick a line on the field. Can you make the ball stop on that line in five kicks? Three? Use the *side of your foot* to propel the ball.

3 CHALLENGE

BOCCI.   Students select partners and put one ball between them. This ball is a **target ball** and is placed ten yards from each partner. Alternating kicks, who can strike the target ball first?

PURSUIT.   Next, partners move ten yards apart. The goal in this activity is to strike #1's ball before #2's is hit. Each partner gets one point each time he or she contacts the partner's ball. Remember, one kick at a time.

4 CLOSER

HOOP GOLF.   Scatter 15–20 hoops around the field. The basic goal in regulation golf is to hit the ball into the targeted hole in as few strokes as possible. Students pick five hoops and see how many *holes in one* they can make.

Name _____

Room _____

SOFT TOSS

One of the most difficult parts of hitting is judging where the ball will cross the plate. Find a partner. Roll up a newspaper and either rubber band the roll or wrap with masking tape. If played inside the house, use a tightly rolled sock.

The pitcher and hitter face each other, with the pitcher kneeling ten feet away directly opposite the hitter's back foot. The pitcher tosses *underhand* and the hitter (in a batter's stance) swings with arms extended. Try to hit only good pitches.

After five hits, batter and pitcher change places.

REACTION TIME

1 WARM-UP

Reaction time is the time it takes you to move once you realize the need to act. This warm-up allows students to react quickly to your cues. Students are arranged in even rows in the middle of the floor. The drill begins with class members **running in place.** When you point (forward, backward, left, right), students react quickly by moving **_three_** quick steps in that direction.

2 CONCEPT

CHAIR DROP.   Distribute one plastic bat, ball (softball size), and chair to each group of three. Chairs are placed 10–15 feet from the wall. Right-handed batters (backs to wall) are situated on the right-hand side of the chairs, left-handed batters on the opposite side. Pitchers stand on the chairs and drop balls over the strike zone. Fielders return balls to the pitcher. Players rotate positions every five pitches.

3 CHALLENGE

AIR HOCKEY.   Arrange mats side by side, four feet apart. Place three to four players on each mat. One chalkboard eraser is distributed to each player. Players lie on stomachs and attempt to strike light plastic hockey pucks or perforated golf balls against the *edge* of their opponent's mat. All contacts must be made with the erasers. (*Credit:* Modified from "Floor Hockey," *Great Activities Newsletter,* May/June 1996, vol. 14, no. 5, p. 35.)

4 CLOSER

BEANBAG DROP.   Partners stand facing two feet apart. Partner #1 holds a beanbag (eye level) and, without warning, drops it in front of partner #2. Partner #2 attempts to catch it before it hits the floor. After three turns, partners switch places. Try it with the receiving hand *held above* the dropping hand.

Name _____

Room _____

NONDOMINANT SIDE

One of the criteria for success in sports is the ability to control objects with both sides of the body. Find a bouncy ball and work on the following _nondominant side_ drills.

CAN YOU:

- place your dominant hand behind you and dribble a ball with the opposite in straight lines and circles?
- dribble the ball in a "V" shape without moving your feet?
- dribble a ball using all sides of your nondominant foot?

STRIKING

MAY

SUNDAY	MONDAY	TUESDAY	WEDNESDAY	THURSDAY	FRIDAY	SATURDAY
Quality Daily Physical Education	*Play a balloon volleyball game over a piece of furniture.*	Find a rubber ball & see how many times you can strike it off a wall using either hand.	**Work on your soccer ball handling skills in a yard or park.**	**Practice dribbling a ball around the block.** Always keep the ball close to you.	*Create a striking game using a palm & a wadded-up paper ball.*	Pretend you are a hockey goalie. Have someone attempt to score on you using a Nerf™ or a wadded-up paper ball.
See if you & a partner can make 10 consecutive alternating hits with a balloon using: Hands. Thighs. Feet.	**How many times in a row can you bounce a small ball with your right hand? Left hand?**	**Pick a target on a wall. How many times out of 10 can you strike a ball into this area?**	**In an open field see HOW FAR you can strike a ball with a bat, racquet, foot or hand.**	**Jog with a partner. Partner 1, in front, throws a ball overhead to partner 2, behind. Partner 2 catches, runs in front & repeats.**	**Have a family "heading" contest. See who can bounce a balloon off his or her head the most times in a row.**	*Lie on your back. Have a family member drop a ball or balloon & practice sending it back with hands or feet.*
Place an empty plastic drink bottle 1' from a wall. Can you knock it over by throwing or kicking?	Play push-up tag. Face a partner in a push-up position and see who can strike the other person's hand 10 times first.	In an open space, play a **"pepper"** batting game where the pitcher tosses to the batter, who taps it right back.	*Wrap a nylon stocking around a reshaped wire coat hanger & practice striking a wadded paper ball upward.*	**Create a home bowling game using empty milk cartons for pins & a rolled-up sock for a ball.**	**Play a game of consecutive completions. 2 people pass to each other while 2 more try to intercept. Dropped balls equals a change of possession.**	**Work on striking a ball to a partner who is on the move.**
Practice striking a rebounding ball off an (outdoor) wall. How many rebounds can you hit in a row?	**Work on a cross-over dribble using rapid hand-to-hand dribbling.**	Find a balloon & practice striking it on the following body parts, in order: head, shoulder, chest, thigh, foot. Repeat.	Talk a family member into guarding you while you dribble a ball with hands and feet.	**Practice striking a balloon or Nerf™ ball right above your hairline continuously.**	**Play a softball game. Do not strike out.**	*Outdoors, work on stationary and running-approach kicks. What makes the ball go farther?*
Partner 1 stands with palms open just above the shoulders. Partner 2, a small ball in each hand, throws the right ball to #1's right hand & the left to #1's left hand. Reverse. Speed up.	**Alternate striking a ball off a wall to a partner 10 feet away. Try to guess where the rebound will take place.**	**Practice dribbling a soft ball slowly through the house without letting it touch a wall.**	Face a partner in a sit-up position. Partner 1 lies back, touches a ball to the floor, raises up, passes ball to partner 2 & completes a second sit-up before receiving it.	QDPE/NPE (reversed)	**"Every Child Deserves Planned, Purposeful P.E."**	

Calendar calisthenics is a voluntary daily fitness supplement conducted outside of school. As homework is completed, parents put a check in the corner box for the day. Small doses of creative exercises can move students toward more consistent exercise patterns. Students will find same mind and muscle activities to provide links between the classroom and gymnasium.

Name _____

Room _____

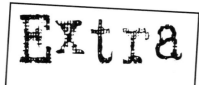  Homework

Spring is a time to play ball. Our national pastime is the sport of baseball. See if you can match the clues in the column on the left with the American and National League teams on the right. Connect the clues with the teams by drawing a line between them. The first one has been completed for you. Have your parents and friends help as much as needed.

Clues	Teams
father figure	Anaheim Angels
past of meet	Los Angeles Dodgers
draft evaders	St. Louis Cardinals
no jockey on this horse	Detroit Tigers
seafarers	New York Mets
red songbird	Seattle Mariners
Beantown Bombers	San Diego Padres
motor cats	Philadelphia Phillies
halos	Houston Astros
lawmen	Boston Red Sox
what's your sign?	Texas Rangers

Return to your P.E. Teacher

DANCE AND RHYTHMS

This section offers different situations for students to practice footwork, create, cooperate, perform, and observe a variety of locomotor, nonlocomoter, and pantomime skills. Following this section, students will better understand the rhythmic relationship associated with sport and dance.

"Each response is my own, no need to copy the rest. I explore a myriad of possibilities, all leading toward success." Bud & Sue Turner

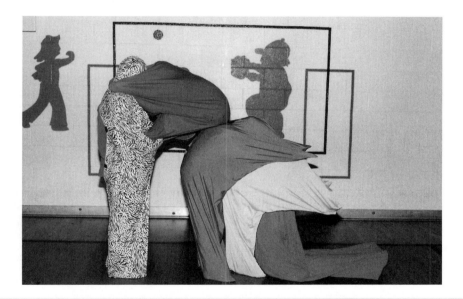

Contents

KEEP THE BEAT

WARM-UP

Select music that has an upbeat 4-count. As a group, practice the following foot patterns:

Count 1	Count 2	Count 3	Count 4
Side straddle	Jump	Jump	Jump
Side straddle	Jump	Kick one leg forward	Jump
Side straddle	Jump	One-quarter turn	Jump
Side straddle	Jump	Your choice	Jump

CONCEPT

Distribute two 1-foot lengths of 3/8- to 1/2-inch dowels to each student. Have students practice striking the ends of each stick two times on the floor and hit together on the third and fourth counts. On the third and fourth beats, CAN YOU CONTACT the sticks:

- in front of you?
- behind your back?
- at your side?
- under your leg?
- above your head?

Can you flip one stick and then the other?

CHALLENGE

Distribute a thin circular elastic band to each group of three students. Two stand inside with the rope at ankle level while the jumper stands in the middle. The two holding the band jump twice with feet apart and twice with feet together. The jumper inside jumps twice inside and twice outside (straddle). Change positions.

CLOSER

FOOT BEAT TAG. Students find their personal space. Four students are designated as taggers and wear pinnies or vests. Each time they hear the drum beat, they take <u>one</u> step. When the drum beats become rapid, runners may move more quickly. If touched by a tagger, students continue to move on the next beat.

Name _____

Room _____

WRIST DANCING

Find a partner and stand arm's-length apart. Slowly fall away before gently pulling each other back to a balanced position. Try falling at different levels and catching with various parts of the arms. Can you dance this way while supporting each other with just one arm?

TWISTER

WARM-UP

A twist is performed when a body part is fixed and the other body parts are turned away. Using the music "Pop Goes the Weasel," students move through general space using a vigorous locomotor pattern, such as skipping. On the word "Pop," they jump high into the air, land, and freeze in a twisted shape. Students try creating shapes at different levels: high, medium, and low.

CONCEPT

Distribute one bath towel to each student. (An ample supply can usually be collected from parents.) Have students stand on top of their towels in a clear space and practice twisting without moving off their towel. Can you twist while:
- on both feet?
- on one foot?
- changing levels?
- moving?
- changing speeds?

CHALLENGE

Using the music "The Twist" by Chubby Checker, students challenge a partner to a wall-to-wall twister race. Students must keep both feet in contact with their towel.

CLOSER

TOWEL TWISTER TAG.   Select four students to be taggers. Taggers carry an object (eraser, rubber chicken, etc.) that is given to anyone they touch. Receivers become new taggers. Using the same "Twist" music, students twist and turn their way across the floor trying to avoid being tagged. All players must keep both feet on their towels.

Name _____

Room _____

Take Home

GRAPEVINE

The pattern below is called the Grapevine. Practice this with members of your family and, when you return to school, we will turn it into an "Achy Breaky" dance.

Grapevine

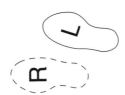

| Step R | Cross L Behind R | Step R | Stomp L Clap Hands |

Scattered Squares

This is a nontraditional way to teach square dance. Instruct each move separately and then combine them. Select a Western tune and call the formations over a microphone, if possible.

1 WARM-UP

CALL: HIT THE TRAIL. Students skip and clap to the beat of the music. Other locomotor movements can be used.

2 CONCEPT

Instruct students to "Do Si Do" (move toward one another, pass back to back, and then move backward to place) with as many individual classmates as they can until the cue "Swing Your Partner" is called. Children perform hooked right-arm swing turns with as many individual class members until the next cue. *Turns should be done one time around and then students need to move on to another classmate.*

3 CHALLENGE

CIRCLE LEFT. Students quickly join into a small circle of 4–6 and begin circling as a group to the left.
CIRCLE RIGHT. Reverse the circle
FLAG POLE. One person from the circle gets down on his or her knees and extends one arm up. The students in the circle place their right hands on the center person's hand (flag pole) and circle clockwise. (**Teacher:** You can call "Switch flag poles.")

4 CLOSER

TRAIN. Students move to the music with their hands on a friend's shoulders. On the call "Catch a train," join another set of partners. When the cue "All Train" is called, the entire class links up. *Students ending up by themselves when partners are required can always make a group of three.*

(Original idea: Karen Hamilton, Cottage Lake Elementary, Bothell, WA.)

Name _____

Room _____

RHYTHMIC GYMNASTICS

This sport includes dance, gymnastics, and the use of small apparatus (balls, hoops, ribbon sticks, clubs). Find a ball and experiment with bouncing, rolling, and tossing while in different positions.

IDEAS:

- roll up and down legs
- catch on different parts
- throw high, catch low

Copy Cat

WARM-UP

Students listen to the beat of the drum and find their own special way to move slowly and then quickly. How closely can you match the movements of a friend? Students take turns being the leader and keep their moves simple.

CONCEPT

Distribute a 4- to 6-foot ribbon to each student. (Ribbons can be fabric or paper.) Students copy the following teacher-directed patterns:

TWIRL:
- at your side
- above your head
- in front of your body
- in a figure-8 motion

Students work in a small group and create their own movements. They take turns being the leader.

CHALLENGE

Select some appropriate music and have each small group create a matching sequence with at least 4 different ribbon moves:
- students can be moving
- stationary
- change levels
- change directions and speed

CLOSER

Videotape the sequences and show students their products.

Name _____

Room _____

MATCH THIS

Take turns being a leader and follower, matching each other's movements as you complete the following activities:

- March side by side.
- Jog side by side.
- Perform push-ups.
- Hop, skip, jump.
- Jump rope.
- Perform jumping jacks.
- Dribble a ball.

PARTNER PUSH-UPS

Find a partner and face each other with heads touching. Practice slow-motion push-ups, moving up and down at the same time. Next, place a small ball or other soft object between your heads and repeat the push-up movement. Can you keep the object between your heads as you move *slowly* sideways?

STOMP

WARM-UP

Scatter hula hoops around the floor. Have students jog around the hoops to the "Bunny Hop." On the 3 beats (hop, hop, hop), students complete that many movements inside the closest hoop. Vary the pattern on subsequent turns, for example, 2 jumps in—1 jump out or jump in—jump out—jump in.

CONCEPT

Distribute one broomstick or similar-size dowel to each student. Using the music "We Will Rock You" by Queen, students practice the following stomp patterns. Holding the broomstick or dowel with two hands, students:
- Hit broom on floor twice, stomp *R* foot (repeat)
- Hit broom on floor twice, stomp *L* foot (repeat)
- Hit broom on floor, stomp *R*, stomp *L*, (repeat)
- Hit broom on floor, stomp *L*, stomp *R*, (repeat)

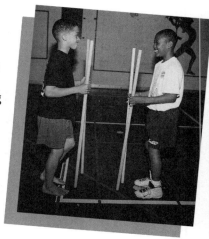

CHALLENGE

The dance described below is called the Teton Mountain Stomp.
Formation: Form a double circle and face your partner. Join hands. Inside partner starts with the opposite foot.
OUTSIDE CIRCLE
- Step out with R; together with L; step out R; stomp L.
- Step out with L; together with R; step out L; stomp R.
- Step out R; stomp L; step out L; stomp R; step out R; stomp L; step out L; stomp R.
- Join inside hands; walk forward counterclockwise 4 counts; turn & join inside hands; walk backward 4 counts.
- Walk forward clockwise 4 counts; turn & join inside hands; walk backward 4 counts.
INSIDE CIRCLE
- Step out with L; together with R; step out L; stomp R.
- Step out with R; together with L; step out R; stomp L.
- Step out L; stomp R; step out R; stomp L; step out L; stomp R; step out R; stomp L.
- Join inside hands; walk forward counterclockwise 4 counts; turn & join inside hands; walk backward 4 counts.
- Walk forward clockwise 4 counts; turn & join inside hands; walk backward 4 counts.
Repeat dance.

CLOSER

Students make up a matching stomp pattern with a partner.

STOMP

This is the name of a rhythmic/dance *show* that is growing in popularity from coast to coast. The cast members use their feet, sticks, garbage can lids, cans, and their imaginations to combine fast-moving foot movements with exciting rhythmic patterns.

Find regular household props to create your own show!

Dancing Through the Decades

WARM-UP

1950S . . . MUSIC: "ROCK AROUND THE CLOCK."
Students select a partner and stand side by side. On the cue "Put your glad rags on. . .," students start jogging for 31 counts. On count 32, they jump and turn to face their partner. They join hands and do the "dishrag" for 8 counts and repeat it in the other direction for 8 counts. Repeat the entire sequence.

CONCEPT

1960S . . . MUSIC: "DO YOU LOVE ME?" Some of the memorable dances of the 1960s were the Twist, Monkey, Jerk, Hand Jive, Swim, Pony, and Mashed Potato. Students pick one of the dance titles. What kinds of movements would you use to bring this dance alive? (This can be done in a small group.) (**Teacher:** You may need to show basic movements and let children explore variations.)

CHALLENGE

1970S . . . MUSIC: "STAYIN' ALIVE." The hustle step was made famous by John Travolta in the movie *Stayin' Alive.* Teach one of the basic steps:
- **Step out to the side on** *right.*
- **Step** *left* **behind** *right.*
- **Step out to the side on** *right.*
- **Kick** *left* **foot forward.**
- **Repeat to the** *left.*

Working in groups of 3 or 4, challenge students to match their steps in their own formation: side by side; in a circle; facing; in a line.

CLOSER

1980S . . . MUSIC: "LET'S GET PHYSICAL." This decade marked the beginning of the Aerobics era. Each student needs two soup cans and practices some of the following arm movements to the music:
- **alternating arm curls**
- **alternating reverse arm curls**
- **hammer curls**
- **forward and lateral shoulder raises**
- **upright rows**

Try jogging in place while doing the arm movements.

Name _____

Room _____

JUGGLING PLASTIC

Juggling is a rhythmic experience where both sides of the body work in unison. Regular juggling equipment is expensive. When you don't have access to scarves, try the following idea.

Most households have plastic grocery bags. Find three and follow the suggested progression below:

One bag:

• Throw in a letter "U" pattern from the dominant to the nondominant side and repeat.

Two bags:

• Throw one from the dominant side first. When it peaks, throw the second bag from the nondominant side and repeat.

Three bags:

• Place two bags in your dominant hand and the third in your nondominant hand. Throw bag #1 from dominant side. As the first bag peaks, throw the bag from the opposite hand (catch the first), and then throw bag #3 from the dominant hand.

CHAIR DANCING

WARM-UP

MUSICAL CHAIRS. Students sit on chairs scattered about the room. One student is randomly selected to remove his or her chair. You call out a locomotor pattern, such as skipping, and following a signal to begin, students skip about the floor. When the music stops, students sit on the remaining chairs. Each person on a chair earns a point. This process continues until five chairs remain. *Students are never eliminated.*

CONCEPT

Select music with a distinct 4-count, e.g., "The Hustle" or "Electric Boogie." Students try the following movements while:

Seated
- March in place.
- Step *left* kick *right,* step *right* kick *left*
- Touch floor and clap.
- Circle arms.
- Create your own.

Standing (holding back)
- Jump in place.
- Straddle jump.
- Step *right* kick *left* to side; step *left* kick *right* to side
- Step *left* touch *right* to back.
- Step *right* touch *left* to back.
- Create your own.

CHALLENGE

CHAIR LINKS. Select a song with a distinct 4-count beat. Arrange half as many chairs as students in a circle with a 3-foot space between. Half the group stands in between while the other half sit on the chairs. All face inward. Students practice the following 4-count pattern while sitting and standing.
- Step *right* - step *left* -step *right* - kick *left*.
- Reverse and repeat.

On your signal, students move clockwise to the next position. They continue to move from place to place until they return to their starting position.

CLOSER

Students sit in chairs arranged in a circle. One student at a time goes to the center and leads the class in a movement selected from the ***Concept***.

Name _____

Room _____

INVISIBLE ROPES

Find a partner, stand side by side, and practice <u>matching</u> two 2-foot jumps. Next, <u>mimic</u> rope swing movements with the wrists.

Create a <u>synchronized</u> routine where:
- One partner follows the other.
- The speed changes from slow to fast to slow.
- Legs move back and forth (the Bell) and side to side (the Skier).

What else is possible?

It's Electric

WARM-UP

This lesson works best with stocking feet and a slippery surface. Students find a personal space and sit down. (**Teacher:** Demonstrate a sliding action.) Have the students stand and practice sliding following your designated directions. On the signal (music), challenge the students to slide carefully to each endline and baseline and return to their personal space before the music stops.

CONCEPT

Teach the "Electric Slide." The steps are illustrated here.

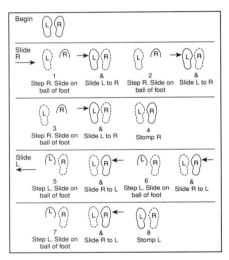

(Credit: *Complete Book of Line Dancing,* Christy Lane, Human Kinetics, 1995.)

CHALLENGE

Can students bounce a ball while performing any of the "Electric Slide" steps?

CLOSER

CIRCUIT BREAKER. Have the students sit in a circle and join hands. Select two students to sit in the center and assign them the job of "circuit breakers." You ask the circuit breakers to close their eyes while one of the circle members is designated as the "starter." On the signal, eyes are opened and the starter begins by squeezing the hand of one of the persons sitting beside him or her. If the circuit breakers identify where the current is, they must change places with the two students in the circle and the game starts over.

Name _____

Room _____

Take Home

TEN

Assume a standing position and try to make ten *equal* downward movements ending in a squat position. Repeat, moving back up. Remember, each movement should be the same.

From a push-up position, move your hands close to your feet in ten *even* movements. Reverse this pattern.

Next, change your even movements to variable rhythm and speed patterns, such as seven quick downward moves and three slow upward moves. Experiment with other combinations (six and four, eight and two, etc.).

THE BEAT IS ON

WARM-UP

Students lie on stomach in a circle with heads facing toward the center. Keep enough space between each student so that they can easily be stepped over. Students start a 3-beat hand rhythm (soft–soft–loud) on the floor. On a signal, one specified student gets up and begins jogging and stepping over each circle member. As he or she passes over a person, that student gets up and follows, etc. Upon returning to their places, they rejoin the circle and continue the beat.

CONCEPT

SPORT ELEPHANT
Music: You need the song "We Will Rock You" by Queen.
Formation: Students sit in a circle facing inward.
Group Size: Five to seven students.
Directions: A sign is placed in front of each student designating a particular sport or activity. King Elephant is the leader. On his or her left is the Showers. Your goal is to become King Elephant and not end up in the showers. Everyone in the circle starts the beat (slap thighs twice—slap hands together). Sport Elephant begins the game by slapping his or her thighs twice—showing his or her sign—slaps thighs twice again and shows the sign of another circle member. When the sign is passed, the receiver slaps his or her thighs twice—shows their sign—slaps thighs twice and shows the sign of a different circle member. This continues until someone shows an incorrect sign or doesn't stay on beat. When this occurs, the student making the mistake moves to the showers and everyone from the shower sign to that person's position moves up one spot; thus some students' signs change. Keep the regular slap, slap, clap beat unless involved in the sending or receiving of a sign. See signs and related movements on the following page.

CHALLENGE

Students try playing the game or showing signs and keeping the beat to a song with a faster or slower pace.

CLOSER

Assign each group a new and different sport and have them develop a sign for it. Have them share it with the other class members.

SPORT ELEPHANT SIGNS AND MOVEMENTS

SPORT ELEPHANT

SHOWERS

SWIMMING

BASKETBALL

FOOTBALL

KARATE

Name _____

Room _____

UNDERLYING BEAT

Try to pick out the underlying beat from a song on the radio, VH1, or MTV. Assume a *push-up* position and try to *slap out* that beat by alternating support hands up and down.

©2000 by Parker Publishing Company

Points of Interest

WARM-UP

Show the students pictures of objects that have pointed edges, such as a diamond, a star, a rectangle, a roof of a house, etc. Have the students visualize themselves in a shape that has many points and then have them express their visualization with their bodies.

- Shapes can be still.
- Shapes can be at different levels.
- Shapes can be in motion.

CONCEPT

Provide the students with a choice of interesting props. These should be objects the children could use to assist them in creating shapes that show pointed edges. Examples might be:

- surgical tubing
- stretch bags
- latex stretch bands
- pieces of dowel
- plastic tubes (golf tubing)
- colored streamers

CHALLENGE

Organize students into groups of 2, 3, or 4. With props of their choice, students design a shape that has multiple "points of interest."

- Shapes can be still.
- Shapes can be moving.

CLOSER

Each group should share its shape with classmates. (**Teacher:** Take photos to further illustrate the concept.) This lesson can be done to explore other types of shapes such as rounded or twisted formations.

Take Home

CHINESE JUMP ROPE

Chinese Jump Rope is a great way to work on rhythm skills. It's inexpensive and an excellent form of exercise.

To start, link 25–50 thick rubber bands together in a circle. Two players step inside and hold the bands around their ankles (shoulder-width apart). Holders stand 3 to 4 feet away from each other. The jumper stands facing one of the turners **outside** the ropes.

Work on mastering the following sequences:

1. <u>Ropes at ankle height</u>
   - Jumper jumps in (both feet) and jumps out.
   - Jumper hops in (one foot) and hops out.
   - Jumper lifts outside rope with foot and steps inside (creating an X) and jumps out.
   - Jumper jumps to landing on both ropes and jumps out.
2. Repeat above sequence with ropes held <u>between ankles and knees</u>.
3. Repeat sequence with ropes at <u>knee height</u>.

JUNE

DANCE AND RHYTHMS

SUNDAY	MONDAY	TUESDAY	WEDNESDAY	THURSDAY	FRIDAY	SATURDAY
CUNPE		I Hear and I Forget. I See and I Remember. I Do and I Understand.		**D**o a hat dance with your favorite hat.	**D**ance with a friend to 2 songs on the radio.	**P**ractice a step aerobic routine over a low stable object.
Practice a new dance step on a bath towel.	**L**ipsync & dance to a TV music video or a song on the radio.	**C**reate a slow-motion dance with a friend.	**C**an you travel while in a rounded or stretched position? Can you balance in these shapes?	*C*reate a new Jive hand routine.	**W**ithout speaking, dance out a request to a parent or a friend.	*M*ake up an "arms only" dance.
Bounce a ball to your favorite song.	*S*ynchronize a hip-hop or line dance with a friend.	Practice moving up & down on 10 distinctive beats. Try different combinations: down 2, up 8, etc.	**M**ake up a dance with movements that sound like these words: Salsa, Cha Cha, and Jerk.	*T*ry these action sentences: Rise, wobble, spin, explode, collapse. Reverse it.	**W**ork on a symmetry dance where both sides of your body work together at the same time.	**M**ake up a sport aerobic routine that incorporates the sports of tennis, basketball, boxing, & speed skating.
Find some old scarves & make up a slow motion juggling routine.	Point your toes in & point your toes out. How fast can you move sideways with this pattern?	*W*ithout touching, mirror a partner's arm & leg movements.	**C**lap to the beat of a song on the radio.	**R**esearch & list 4 different dances from 4 different countries.	**A**sk a parent, relative, or neighbor to teach you a dance from the past. Who taught you?	**F**ind a slippery floor. Put on some socks & practice sliding your legs in & out. Add some music & slide.
With a real or imaginary jump rope, jump to your favorite song.	**U**sing a small space, perform a "phone booth" dance.	**D**o an aerobic routine using 3 locomotor movements, slide, hop, skip, jump, etc.	*W*hat can you do with other dance forms such as ballet? Jazz? Modern?	**D**evelop a dance that students in wheelchairs could perform.		PE4KIDS

Calendar calisthenics is a voluntary daily fitness supplement conducted conducted outside of school. As homework is completed, parents put a check in the corner box for the day. Small doses of creative exercises can move students toward more consistent exercise patterns. Students will find some mind and muscle activities to provide links between the classroom and gymnasium.

Name _____

Room _____

List ten dances that move like they "sound."
How many can you do? (Sample: Robot)

1. _____

2. _____

3. _____

4. _____

5. _____

6. _____

7. _____

8. _____

9. _____

10. _____

Return to your P.E. Teacher

JULY

HOW QUICK R U?

SUNDAY	MONDAY	TUESDAY	WEDNESDAY	THURSDAY	FRIDAY	SATURDAY
	"Prevent couch potatoes while they're still small fries."			ZIG ZAG JUMP!		Find a partner. #1 holds a tennis ball (palms down). #2 places his or her hand on top. Without warning, the ball is dropped and #2 attempts to catch it (with the top hand) before it hits the ground.
Find a partner. #1 holds a soccer ball or basketball on the back of #1's neck. Without warning, the ball is dropped & #1 attempts to catch it. Can you clap your hands before catching?	Find a partner. #1 holds the top end of a dollar bill. Without touching, #2 places index finger & thumb near the bottom. Without warning, #1 drops & #2 attempts to catch it before the president's picture.	Place a yardstick or 3-foot piece of tape on the floor. How many side-to-side jumps can you make over the line in 60 seconds? Challenge a friend!	Find 6 paper or plastic cups and see how quickly you can upstack and downstack them in a pyramid pattern.	Stand facing a partner & interlock fingers. Who can be the first to touch the partner's feet with his or her foot 10 times?	Place small pieces of tape (1 foot apart) on the floor in the pattern above. How quickly can you touch each spot while hopping on 1 foot? Time yourself.	Work on jumping high in the air & touching your toes. Can you touch when legs are pointed forward? Apart?
Practice bouncing a ball. Can you perform 3 push-ups before it comes to a stop? Five? Ten?	If you can make a full turn when you jump in the air, that's a 360° jump. Focus on an object & see if you can rotate past that object.	Place a tennis ball between your ankles, jump, release & catch. Can you roll it out in front, jump, trap, release & catch?	Time yourself when tying your shoes.	How quickly can you move a basketball between your legs in a circle-8 pattern?	Practice jumping in the air & click your heels together. What is the highest number of clicks you can make while in the air?	Face a wall & stretch your hands upward. Place a small piece of tape 1 foot above your fingertips. How many times can you touch the tape in 1 minute?
A good time in the 40-yard dash is an excellent measurement of speed. A good time is 4.5 seconds for a pro. What's your time? _____ seconds.	Starting from the foul line, dribble to the hoop, shoot until you make it, return to the foul line & repeat. How many times can you score in 60 seconds? The average for the Atlanta Hawks was 16.	Place 2 markers 30' apart. Practice moving from marker to marker in a shuffle motion without crossing your feet. How many seconds does it take to touch the markers 5 times?	Blow up a balloon (size of softball), hold it above your head & release. Can you catch it before it hits the ground?	Fingertip exchange: Hold 1 small beanbag in the palm of your throwing hand and 1 on top of your thumb & index finger. Toss both into the air & reverse the positions.	Practice dribbling 2 balls at the same time. Can you move & maintain control? Can you cross over?	Practice throwing a ball through your legs & catch behind. How quickly can you throw & still catch? Can you reverse the direction?
Place a beanbag on top of your head. Tilt your head & try to catch it on your foot.	How quickly can you solve this riddle? If one is three and three is five, what is four? Answer _____	Find a safe grassy area & challenge someone to a "backward race."	How many jump rope speed jumps can you do in 10 seconds?	Face a partner in a push-up position. Who can be the first to touch their partner's hands 10 times? All contacts must be made from the UP position.	Find an old car tire (or similar weighted object). Tie a rope around it & practice sprinting while pulling it behind.	Sit facing a partner, legs crossed, hands on knees 2' apart. Place a ball or beanbag between partners. Alternate saying "Right or left. Who can pick up first?"
Use a basketball or soccer ball & practice alternating toe touches on top.	Throw 3 small balls into the air. Can you catch all 3?					

Calendar calisthenics is a voluntary daily fitness supplement conducted outside of school. As homework is completed, parents put a check in the corner box for the day. Small doses of creative exercises can move students toward more consistent exercise patterns. Students will find some mind and muscle activities to provide links between the classroom and gymnasium.

EXERCISING BY THE NUMBERS

AUGUST

SUNDAY	MONDAY	TUESDAY	WEDNESDAY	THURSDAY	FRIDAY	SATURDAY
Children are 25% of our population and 100% of our future.						Throw & hit a target 5 times in a row.
Run in place for 6 minutes.	Perform 7 different stretches while on your back.	Play a game of catch with a friend. Can you catch 8 in a row?	"9" in German means NO. How many laps can you jog around your house with no stops?	Perform 10 push-ups while your head is above & then below your feet.	From a sitting position, legs 12" apart, spend 11 minutes trying to stretch fingertips past your heels.	Jump a real or imaginary rope 12 times your age.
Do 13 (slow) stretches with arms & legs spread apart.	Try to complete 14 bent-knee sit-ups in 30 seconds.	Balance on one foot at a time for 15 seconds.	Perform 16 wall push-ups.	Practice 17 cartwheels alternating left and right sides.	Practice bouncing a ball between your legs 18 times.	In a one-hour TV program do 19 jumping jacks during each commercial break.
Find a step & step up & down 20 times with your right foot & then your left foot.	Perform 21 vertical power jumps, trying to get higher on each jump.	Perform 22 zigzag jumps in four different directions.	Hold a push-up position for 23 seconds from three different positions.	Practice your handstands. How many does it take to total 24 balanced seconds?	Measure off 25'. How many standing (2') jumps does it take to cover 25'?	Have 2 people hold a string (horizontally) 26" off the floor. Is anyone able to Limbo under?
Go on a 27-minute plus walk with your family.	How many seconds does it take to throw & catch a ball off a wall 28 times?	Write down 29 activities you can do to improve your health.	Raise your heart rate 30 beats a minute and keep it there for 15 minutes.	PASS UNDER	LIMBO	

Calendar calisthenics is a voluntary daily fitness supplement conducted outside of school. As homework is completed, parents put a check in the corner box for the day. Small doses of creative

Part Two

Games

Games, as the central lesson content, are passe' in the "NEW" physical education. The following 43 games include *Cooperation, Aerobic,* and *Academic* (Thinking) activities.

The majority of these activities are short term, fun, skill-oriented, and adaptable. They are an integral part of a carefully designed lesson, but not the single focus.

Eliminating Elimination

Too many kids play too many games

the outcome of which is often the same.

The strong finish first while second is last,

success is a dream, losers harassed.

The solution is simple just follow this rule:

eliminate elimination in every school.

—Bud Turner

LET'S LEARN SOME NEW GAMES

It's hard to improve
when we're all standing still
watching the first picks
gain all the skill.

Let's learn some new games
where no one complains
there are too many rules
too long to explain.

Let's learn some new games
we can play at home
along with some neighbors
and when we're alone.

Let's learn some new games
that makes us ALL go,
yet the teacher says
that's all she/he knows.

Bud Turner

COOPERATION GAMES

These games are basically noncompetitive and challenge both small and large groups to work together to accomplish a common goal. Cooperative games reinforce a positive learning environment by:

- Eliminating elimination
- Reducing the "win at all cost" syndrome
- Teaching students to view situations from others' perspectives
- Encouraging higher-level reasoning skills

ACTIVITY

Through the Black Hole

CONCEPT

COOPERATION

EQUIPMENT

1 36-inch hula hoop for each pair

DESCRIPTION

This cooperative activity challenges partners to alternately roll and scoot through a moving hoop. On an open field, partner #1 places his or her hand on the top of the hoop, and rolls it slowly forward. Partner #2 runs alongside and tries to slip through it before the hoop touches the ground. Once both can successfully move through, they can challenge another set of partners to see who can score the most pass-throughs while moving from one end of the field to the other.

MODIFICATION

• Increase the size of the hoops.

ACTIVITY

The Crossing

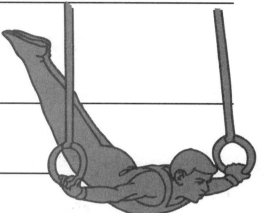

CONCEPT

COOPERATION

EQUIPMENT

4 foldable mats; large bucket
of tennis balls; 4 automobile tires,
3-foot 2×4s; 4 Frisbee™ discs; 4 stopwatches

DESCRIPTION

Divide the class into groups of five or six. Tell students the ferry boat has run aground and to get across the river (gym), they can improvise using one of the four different methods:

TRACTOR: Attach three foldable mats with Velcro™ ends into one circular unit. Students get on hands and knees and crawl, moving the tractor across the gym. If the mats separate, simply reattach and continue from that point.

LILY PADS: Place Frisbee™ discs at one end of the floor. Each group member stands on one pad and, without stepping on the floor, moves across by doubling up and sliding the extra pad forward. Students stepping off a pad must be rescued.

BRIDGES: Like the Lily Pad, auto tires and 2×4 boards are fashioned in such a way to permit team members to cross without touching the floor.

THE RAFT: Place tennis balls under a foldable mat. Team members get onboard and push the mat forward with hands. As balls come out the back, they are handed to the front players who replace them under the forward section of the raft.

MODIFICATION

- Give time cards and stopwatches to each team to measure their progress.

One-Minute Madness

CONCEPT

COOPERATION

EQUIPMENT

1 basketball-sized ball per group of 3

DESCRIPTION

Threesomes form triangles 10 feet apart. Following a signal to begin, groups attempt to exchange the ball by passing in the following order for one minute. Teams quickly sit down after completing the fifth round.

- Round 1: two-hand (underhand) pass
- Round 2: chest pass (no bounce)
- Round 3: chest bounce pass
- Round 4: lateral pass
- Round 5: overhead pass

MODIFICATION

- Execute passes in clockwise and counterclockwise directions.

ACTIVITY

Waterfall

CONCEPT

COOPERATION

EQUIPMENT

2 large garbage bags; 1 soccer-sized ball per group of 4

DESCRIPTION

Place students in groups of four. **Pair #1** stands against a sidewall holding the ends of a garbage bag with a soccer-sized ball in the middle. **Pair #2** stands shoulder to shoulder with **pair #1** holding the receiving bag at waist level.

Following a signal to begin, **pair #1** lets their ball drop into the receiving bag. **Pair #1** moves _under_ that bag and prepares to receive it in their own bag. Dropped balls force a team to return to the starting line and start over.

This process continues until the foursome reaches the opposite sidewall.

MODIFICATION

• Guesstimate how many exchanges it will take to reach the other side. Time teams.

Three in a Row

CONCEPT _____

COOPERATION

EQUIPMENT _____

1 basketball-sized ball for every 6 students

DESCRIPTION _____

Divide into groups of six. Number off (1 to 6). Team #1 is made up of players 1 to 3 and team #2 consists of players 4 to 6. Distribute a basketball-sized ball to each member of team #1. Following a signal to begin, players from team #1 attempt to complete **three** consecutive passes without an interception. Team #2 guards team #1 players and attempts to steal or force an incomplete pass. Turnovers result in the defensive team taking control. How many consecutive passes can you complete? Encourage all players to be on the move.

MODIFICATION _____

- Play with a variety of equipment.
- Implement a time factor.
- Have threesomes complete three consecutive passes and then sit down.

ACTIVITY

Soccer Square Pin Down

CONCEPT

COOPERATION

EQUIPMENT

1 soccer ball; piece of chalk; markers for each square

DESCRIPTION

Arrange students in groups of eight. Draw a 20-foot wide square in chalk and place three to four pins, yarn spools, or empty 2-liter plastic bottles in the middle. Four players begin on defense standing inside the square. The other four are located on the outside corners of the square and pass and kick the ball in an attempt to knock down two of the markers.

Offensive players may not step inside the square and defensive players can't step out. Encourage both teams to move to the ball. The ball is returned to the offense after each defensive steal, missed pass, or kick. Once two of the markers are knocked over, teams change places.

MODIFICATION

• Add a ball for each offensive player.

ACTIVITY

Tanks

CONCEPT

COOPERATION

EQUIPMENT

2 long lines of mats

DESCRIPTION

Divide the class in half. Students lie on stomachs, shoulder to shoulder, facing the same direction at one end of the mat. Following a signal to begin, the first person in both lines rolls over each person and takes his or her place snuggly at the end of his or her line. Upon reaching this position, that player yells "GO" and the next person completes the same process. This continues until all players have rolled across. Which tank line can complete the sequence first?

MODIFICATION

- Add a wave effect by having lying players rock back and forth on shoulders as the rolling player passes over.
- Allow students to roll one after another.

ACTIVITY

Jumping Jack Soccer

CONCEPT

COOPERATION

EQUIPMENT

1 Nerf™, rubber, or soccer-sized ball per group of 3

DESCRIPTION

Number off in groups of three. Players #1 and #2 face five feet apart. Partner #3 stands in the middle and performs *slow-motion* jumping jacks. The passing partners attempt to exchange the ball back and forth between the legs of the jumper. Rotate positions every 60 seconds. Using the inside of your foot, how many goals can you score between rotations?

MODIFICATION

• Change the type of pass.

ACTIVITY

Squares

CONCEPT

COOPERATION

EQUIPMENT

1 soccer-sized ball and 4 cones for each group of 4 students

DESCRIPTION

Students place cones in a square formation 20–30 feet apart. Team members number off ("1," "2," "3," and "4").

Player #1 kicks the ball directly to #2 and follows the ball to that corner. Player #2 traps the ball and passes the ball to #3. How long does it take to return to your starting position? Compete with another team(s) to see who can return and sit down first.

MODIFICATION

- Try different types of kicks.
- Kick in different patterns.
- Use different equipment.

ACTIVITY

Dribble Down

CONCEPT

COOPERATION

EQUIPMENT

1 basketball-sized ball for
each group of 4

DESCRIPTION

Students team up in lines of four,
shoulder to shoulder (arm's-length
apart). The first person in line obtains
a ball, dribbles one to three times,
and bounces to the second
person. This process continues
until the ball reaches the end of the
line. Can you move the ball from one end to the other in eight
bounces? Six? Four? Change directions so you are using your opposite
hand. Try racing another team. As soon as the ball leaves your hand,
sit down. Which team can sit first?

MODIFICATION

- Try exchanging the ball under your legs.
- Try passing while the foursome moves downcourt. After a player
  touches the ball, she or he runs to the back of the line.
- Try passing down while in a push-up position.

Cooperative Hoop Soccer

CONCEPT

COOPERATION

EQUIPMENT

30- to 36-inch hoop and 1
soccer-sized ball for each group of 3

DESCRIPTION

Teams of three get inside their hoop and
place it at hip level. Players inside number
off "one, two, three." The goal in this activity
is to work together while:

- Dribbling the ball (feet) off all four walls and returning to home
  base.
- Alternating kicks between players (in order) as you touch all four
  walls.
- Setting a speed record.

MODIFICATION

- Add a second and third ball.

Co-op Soccer Pop

CONCEPT

COOPERATION

EQUIPMENT

2 to 3 chalked circles 20 inches in diameter; 1 soccer-sized ball for each student; 6 to 10 empty 2-liter plastic bottles per circle

DESCRIPTION

Arrange students evenly in groups of six to ten on the outside of their circle. Each student traps the ball under one foot. Following a signal to begin, players kick toward the targets inside, attempting to knock down all of the markers. Once a ball is kicked, it becomes a FREE ball available to any other teammates to kick back. Players may run after loose balls but all target kicks must be delivered **outside** the circle. The game ends when all of the pins are down and each player has a ball trapped under one foot.

MODIFICATION

- Play for a specific amount of time.
- Use only selected kicks.

The Big Squeeze

CONCEPT

COOPERATION

EQUIPMENT

50+ balloons; 6–8 large boxes or garbage cans

DESCRIPTION

Place students in groups of four behind a common start line. Individual team boxes are placed directly across on a finish line 30–50 feet away. Following a signal to begin, a designated "loader" from each team places a balloon between his or her team members' backs, hips, or stomachs so that each player (including the "loader") is in contact with the balloon. Without the use of hands, teams must keep the balloon from touching the floor as it is transported to a container. Once the balloon is successfully placed in the team box, members return and the "loader" loads TWO balloons. The big squeeze continues by adding an additional balloon after each successful delivery. Dropped balloons must be returned to the start line and reloaded. How many balloons can your team transport in five minutes?

MODIFICATION

• Use different body parts each trip.

AEROBIC GAMES

These games elevate heart rates through continuous exercise and, because of their fast pace, are of shorter duration than the other games in this section. Aerobic games camouflage the hard work that often causes students to drop out of traditional games.

Symptoms of heart disease can begin early in life. Adding aerobic games that are of high interest will encourage children to participate and help to eliminate the onset of heart disease.

ACTIVITY

Beat the Clock

CONCEPT

AEROBIC

EQUIPMENT

Flags or dust cloths for half
the class; stopwatch; wastepaper basket

DESCRIPTION

Divide the class in half and line them up on opposite goal
lines of a football or soccer field. One team attaches an 18-inch flag
on either a belt or in a pocket. Flags may not be tied or held by the
runner and should be displayed at a minimum of 12 inches.
Following a signal to begin, the team without flags chases its flag-
bearing opponents within the established boundaries. Each time a
flag is captured, that player runs it directly to the container situated
next to the instructor at midfield. Players who are stripped of their
flag sit in a single line behind the container. If all flags have not been
captured after one minute, the first person in line takes a flag from
the container and reenters play. The team collecting all of the flags
in the shorter period wins a point.

MODIFICATION

• Designate a certain number of flags to be collected or a specific
time for each team.

ACTIVITY

Gotcha

CONCEPT

AEROBIC

EQUIPMENT

1 beanbag per student

DESCRIPTION

Students obtain a beanbag and find an open space on the floor. Following the signal to begin, students begin moving freely, attempting to *slide* their beanbag into the feet of other class members. Once a player is struck on the foot area, he or she performs a predetermined stunt (jumping jacks, push-ups, etc.) and immediately rejoins the action. Players may *not be hit* while performing their penalty. All beanbags are free to take once on the floor and players are encouraged to run, dodge, and jump away from approaching beanbags.

MODIFICATION

• Accumulate as many "gotchas" (beanbags) as possible within a specified time frame.

Credit: Alternative Sports and Games for the New Physical Education by Bud Turner & Sue Turner (Ginn Press, 1989).

Full-Field Capture the Flag

CONCEPT

AEROBIC

EQUIPMENT

27 18-inch strips of cloth for half the class; 1 stopwatch

DESCRIPTION

Divide the class in half and distribute flags to one team. Flag carriers stuff them in a pocket, belt, or collar with the excess showing a minimum of 18 inches. Flags cannot be tied to other articles of clothing nor can they be guarded by the runner. Following the signal, the chase team attempts to capture and turn over to the instructor a predetermined number of the other team's flags; for example, the tenth flag collected stops the clock. Teams then change places. Boundary lines should be understood prior to the beginning of play.

MODIFICATION

- Play until all flags are collected and turned over to the instructor.
- Place a container in the middle of the field. Players able to beat the flag stealer to the container regain their flag.
- Those losing their flags may *passively* block opponents.

ACTIVITY

Quick Feats

CONCEPT

AEROBIC

EQUIPMENT

1 beanbag for each set of partners

DESCRIPTION

Partners face at midcourt with a beanbag in between. The beanbag symbolizes a trophy that is moved to the winner's side following each event.

EVENTS:
- Stand back to back. On "GO," race your partner to the opposite endline, return, and sit down.
- Be the first to perform 15 jumping jacks.
- Balance the longest on one foot.
- Give five different students high-fives.
- Touch four walls.

MODIFICATION

- Try applicable feats while dribbling a ball.

ACTIVITY

Heads or Tails

CONCEPT

AEROBIC

EQUIPMENT

Pennies for half the class; tape
or chalk; cones

DESCRIPTION

Using tape or chalk, make a line down
the middle of the gym or playground.
Place traffic cones as shown in the
illustration below, 20–30 feet apart on
each side of the midline. Cones
serve as a goal line for runners.

Distribute one penny to each set of partners who stand facing on
opposite sides of the midline. Designate one side as "heads" and the
other side as "tails." Players alternate flipping a coin and letting it
fall to the floor. If heads appears, that partner attempts to tag his or
her opponent before the opponent can retreat across the safety line.
One point is awarded for each legal tag or successful run.

Note: If the game is played inside, place goal lines a safe distance
from the sidewalls.

safety or
goal line
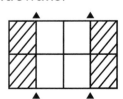
safety or
goal line

MODIFICATION

None.

ACTIVITY

Shipwreck

CONCEPT

AEROBIC

EQUIPMENT

four wall signs

DESCRIPTION

Students stand on a line. The instructor calls out one of the illustrated actions. The last person to complete the task runs to the "Brig." Students assigned to the Brig are automatically free after three calls. The duration of this activity depends upon the group's endurance. Five to ten minutes is usually long enough. Make the calls quickly. The first four directions can be printed on tag board and taped to the wall. Parallel bars or a corner mat make a good brig.

CALLS

BOW

Front of ship

STERN

Back of ship

PORT

Left Side

STARBOARD

Right Side

BRIG

SHIP'S JAIL

OTHER CALLS

MATES in the GALLEY

Three people sitting, holding hands.

HIT THE DECK

Lie on the floor on stomach.

ABANDON SHIP

Two partners holding hands, rowing in sitting position.

ROLL CALL

3 rows of 5 people standing at attention in 3 designated lines.

Credit: Alternative Sports and Games for the New Physical Education by Bud Turner & Sue Turner (Ginn Press, 1989).

ACTIVITY

Shake the Snake

CONCEPT

AEROBIC

EQUIPMENT

1 jump rope for each set of partners

DESCRIPTION

The partner assigned a rope holds it (lightly) in one hand between the thumb and the index finger. Following a signal to begin, "snake shakers" *run* pulling the slithering strands behind them. At least half the rope should touch the ground. "Snake stompers" attempt to step on the end causing the shaker to lose his or her grip. When this occurs, the stomper and shaker switch roles and the action continues.

MODIFICATION

• Allow partners to go after any snake.

ACTIVITY

File Exchange

CONCEPT

AEROBIC

EQUIPMENT

4 Nerf™ footballs; 4 traffic cones

DESCRIPTION

Place a traffic cone or marker approximately six feet from each corner in the gym. Divide the class into equal groups behind each cone. Distribute a Nerf™ football to players in the front of each line. Following a signal to begin, the first players run to the middle, pass diagonally to the next player in line, and run to the end of that line. Passers and receivers score a point if the ball is caught. How many individual points can you earn?

MODIFICATION

None.

ACTIVITY

Partner Basketball Keep-away

CONCEPT

AEROBIC

EQUIPMENT

1 basketball or volleyball-sized ball for each set of partners

DESCRIPTION

Following a signal to begin, partner #1 starts bouncing his or her ball without committing a *double dribble* or *traveling*. Balls can be bounced anywhere in the gym. Partner #2 attempts to steal the ball <u>without</u> fouling. Each time a legal exchange is made, the partner taking control gains a point. How many points can you score in one minute?

MODIFICATION

- Dribble with one hand behind your back.
- Steal any ball.

ACTIVITY

The Great Escape

CONCEPT

AEROBIC

EQUIPMENT

4 traffic cones; pinnies or vests for taggers

DESCRIPTION

Divide students into five separate groups. One group stands in the middle of the floor (pinnies) while the other four move to separate corners. Following the "GO" signal, students in each corner attempt to escape to a different location without being tagged by one of the students guarding the middle. Runners may simply run along a wall or cut diagonally across the middle. Runners have 10 seconds to leave their corner after they hear "GO." (**Scoring**: Since there are no teams, points are scored individually. Each time a runner escapes safely to a different corner, she or he gains one point. Taggers score a point for each runner tagged. Rotate the tagging group to a corner after five calls.)

MODIFICATION

- Use birthdays instead of the "GO" signal.
- Award an extra point to the corner with the most runners.
- Runners double their point total after successfully touching all four corners.
- Have runners dribble a ball.

ACTIVITY

International Run

CONCEPT

AEROBIC

EQUIPMENT

None.

DESCRIPTION

Players are organized in shuttle lines of five 50–100 feet apart. Students are assigned numbers in one line 1–5 and the opposite line 6–10. Following a signal to begin, player #1 runs to the opposite line, says his or her number (in Spanish), e.g., "uno," and grabs #2, who says "dos." These two students run hand in hand to connect with #3, who says "tres." This process continues with each successive player shouting the correct number in the selected language until all runners are connected. Upon completion, runners line up in a single line calling out their personal number as they sit down.

MODIFICATION

- Use another language.
- Alternate positions in line.

S.L.A.P. (Sequential Learning Aerobic Play)

CONCEPT

AEROBIC

EQUIPMENT

1 cone or other marker per set
of partners

DESCRIPTION

Students face a partner with a
marker between. This activity
calls for quick reactions to
teacher cues. Every action
starts with hands on shoulders
and every sequence ends with
the quicker partner slapping over
the marker. Following the "GO" signal, students compete with their
partner to see who can complete the sequence first. On "GO:"

- Clap hands twice—knock over marker.
- Clap hands twice—perform a jumping jack—knock over marker.
- Clap hands twice—perform a jumping jack—complete a
  360-degree jump turn—do a sit-up—knock over marker.
- Clap hands twice—perform a jumping jack—complete a
  360-degree turn—do a sit-up—touch four walls—knock over
  marker.

MODIFICATION

- Add dribbling to the tasks.

Credit: Bonnie Hopper, National Elementary Teacher of the Year, Billings, MT.

ACTIVITY

Stock Exchange

CONCEPT

AEROBIC

EQUIPMENT

2 boxes of poker chips
(blue, white and red)

DESCRIPTION

Place students in three
separate groups around the
gym. Distribute a variety of different colored chips to each group. On
"GO," students begin running and tagging other classmates. Each
time a tag occurs, players EXCHANGE STOCKS (chips). Action continues
until the "stop" signal is given. Students return to their original group
and place their chips in the same colored groups. The instructor then
announces the dollar value of each stock. (*Sample*: Blue = $15 each;
red = $10 each; white = $5 each.) Once the tabulations are
completed, students pick up their chip and begin a new game.

MODIFICATION

• Alternate chip value.
• Give stocks specific names, e.g., Boeing, Microsoft, etc.

Credit: Cindy Wright and Joe Mushock, Seward Elementary School, Auburn, NY. *Great
Activities Newsletter,* "Game of Chance," Vol. 14, No. 1, p. 31.

ACTIVITY

Bridge Tag

CONCEPT

AEROBIC

EQUIPMENT

3 pinnies

DESCRIPTION

Designate (with pinnies) three students as taggers. Remaining students stand in their personal space awaiting a signal to begin. On "GO," students run, attempting to avoid being tagged. Tagged students *freeze* in a push-**up** (bridge) position. These players may reenter as soon as another player can crawl under their bridge. Rotate taggers every one to two minutes.

MODIFICATION

- Tagged players perform exercises until freed, e.g., jumping jacks, jog in place, etc.

ACTIVITY

Dead Ball

CONCEPT

AEROBIC

EQUIPMENT

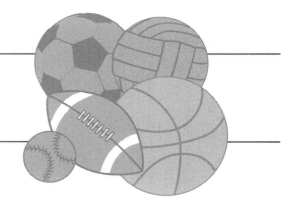

1 bouncy ball per group of 3

DESCRIPTION

Number off players in groups of three. Teams attempt to answer the challenges in each of the three rounds below before their ball dies.

ROUND 1: Player #1 bounces the ball high in the air; **Player #2** completes 15 jumping jacks, while **Player #3** runs to a designated spot 30–50 feet away and returns before the ball dies.

ROUND 2: Player #2 bounces the ball forcefully and all players attempt to run under without touching before it dies.

ROUND 3: Player #3 spins the ball and all three attempt to run around it (1–3 times) before the ball dies.

Repeat each round allowing every player to handle the ball.

MODIFICATION

None.

ACADEMIC GAMES

These games teach traditional academic concepts through movement. While they are most attractive to children whose learning style is *mostly kinesthetic,* all students will benefit from this different learning approach regardless of their learning style.

The following games focus on mathematics skills, traffic safety, prepositions, understanding time, food groups, sequencing, and other skills integral to a comprehensive education. The activities provide the motivation for many students to understand these often difficult concepts for the first time.

Five Food Groups

CONCEPT

ACADEMIC (Nutrition)

EQUIPMENT

Deck of laminated food group
cards including 12–15 separate samples
per group plus an "extra" group (syrup,
cookies, pie, etc.)

DESCRIPTION

Groups of three to five students are
arranged along different points of the gym
floor perimeter or running track. Each team is designated as either
the: **grain, vegetable, fruit, protein, dairy,** or **extra food group.**
Following a signal to begin, groups jog or power walk together
around the running course. Each time players pass the "dealer(s),"
they take one card. The goal is to collect 5 food samples that belong
in their specific group. Once this occurs, they stop running and cheer
on the remaining teams from mid-field. Teams are encouraged to
talk about their selections as they run.

MODIFICATION

None.

ACTIVITY

Odd and Even Tag

CONCEPT

ACADEMIC *(Odd and Even Numbers)*

EQUIPMENT

2 large 1-inch foam dice; 2 traffic cones

DESCRIPTION

Divide the class in half. Teams face each other at midcourt 10 feet apart. One team is designated **ODD** and the other **EVEN.** The teacher stands between the groups and rolls the dice one at a time. If the sum is **ODD,** the odd team chases the even team toward its end of the wall. If the sum is **EVEN,** the even team chases the odd group. For safety, cones are placed 10 feet from each endwall. Chased players making it past their cone are safe. Tagged players simply become members of the team that tagged them.

MODIFICATION

- As students advance in skill, subtraction and multiplication may come into play.
- With K–1 students, place colors over the numbers or use one die.

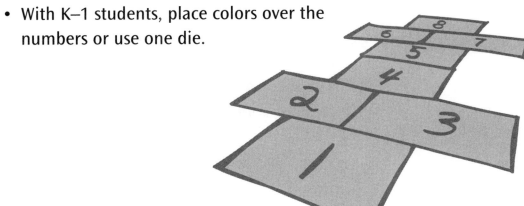

Giant Marbles

CONCEPT

ACADEMIC (Force, Strategies)

EQUIPMENT

2 playground balls per set of partners

DESCRIPTION

Distribute two rubber playground balls to each set of partners. Partners face from opposite sidewalls and number off (1, 2).

The object of the game is to alternately roll and hit the partner's ball before his or her own ball is struck. *Encourage partners to make strategic (small) rolls until they are close enough to strike.*

All rolls are executed with one hand on top of the ball. Balls may not be picked up. Once a ball is hit, play stops and partners return to their sidewalls.

MODIFICATION

- **Marbles Free-for-All.** Players roll at any close ball. Play is nonstop with individual points kept.

Hurry-Up Human Checkers

CONCEPT

ACADEMIC (Higher-Level Thinking Skills)

EQUIPMENT

Chalked out grid or stenciled mats with 18- to 24-inch squares

DESCRIPTION

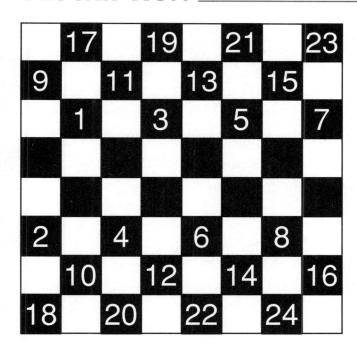

As many as 24 students can play this game at one time; 12 students are designated red and 12 are black. Every five seconds four numbers are called from each team, e.g. 1, 2, 3, 4. When possible, they move toward the opposite end of the board. Players unable to move simply hold until their number is called again. When an opportunity to jump arises, the player may leap-frog an opponent or simply walk around. Which team can move more players across the board?

MODIFICATION

- Have a jumped player jog around the perimeter.
- Play for a specific amount of time.

Emphysema

CONCEPT

ACADEMIC (Restricted
Airway Simulation)

EQUIPMENT

Thin drinking straws

DESCRIPTION

Emphysema is a disease that
narrows the airways, making
breathing difficult. Chronic
smokers often die as a result of
this condition. Videos and movies are full of young people smoking.
To simulate the dangers of this disease, distribute a thin drinking
straw to each student. Have them place the straw in their mouth and
hold their nose with two fingers.

TASKS:
- Jog in place for 10 seconds.
- Walk around the gym.
- Sit down and stand up 5 times.

These tasks should be enough to illustrate the difficulties
emphysema patients experience each day.

MODIFICATION

- Use thinner coffee straws (stirrers) to increase the difficulty.

ACTIVITY

Hop-It

CONCEPT

ACADEMIC (Numbered Sequences)

EQUIPMENT

1 sheet of 4-foot by 6-foot (light) colored vinyl

DESCRIPTION

This game works best as a station in a rotating circuit of activities. Two sets of numbers (1–20) and two sets of mathematical symbols are spread across the vinyl. Tasks for students may include:

Can you hop out your—

- telephone number?
- home address?
- age three different ways?
- age using six different numbers?

MODIFICATION

None.

Movement Prepositions

CONCEPT

ACADEMIC (Understanding Prepositions)

EQUIPMENT

Hula hoops; beams; foldable mats; jump ropes

DESCRIPTION

Divide the class into groups of 3–4 and have them design their own obstacle courses. Regardless of how the equipment is set up, students negotiate each piece in the following ways:

HOOPS = step ***through***

JUMP ROPES = jump ***over***

FOLDABLE MATS = step ***between***

BEAM = walk ***across*** (one side to the other)

MODIFICATION

• Combine the obstacle course with another group's.

ACTIVITY

Get Healthy!

CONCEPT

ACADEMIC (Classification)

EQUIPMENT

100 cards

DESCRIPTION

On one side of 50 cards write the name of a different junk food, e.g., candy bar, soda, chocolate cake, etc. On the other 50 cards, print healthier alternatives, such as carrot, apple, broccoli, etc. To assist younger students, circle the junk foods.

Students are arranged in lines of three along one sideline. Cards are scattered face down across the floor. Following a signal to begin, the first person in each line runs out and turns over **one** card. If the card is a healthy choice, it is returned to the head of that team's line. Junk foods are replaced (face down) and that player returns empty handed and tags the next player in line. Only **one card** can be picked up per trip. The teams collecting more than eight healthy choices in two minutes gain a point.

MODIFICATION

• Designate certain food groups.

ACTIVITY

NerFacts

CONCEPT

ACADEMIC (Spelling Words)

EQUIPMENT

For each group: 1 Nerf™ football
and 1 list of class spelling words

DESCRIPTION

Arrange students in small circles of six.
Distribute one Nerf™ football and weekly list of
spelling words to each group. One player
holds the ball, and calls a spelling word and the name of a second
player in the circle. If the word is spelled correctly, the ball is passed
to that person. Each time a word is correctly spelled, the ball is
passed. Six competitions in a row score a touchdown. Which group
can score six completions?

MODIFICATION

• This game can be used for facts about history, math, science, etc.

ACTIVITY

What Time Is It?

CONCEPT

ACADEMIC (Time)

EQUIPMENT

12 rubber markers (vinyl poly/spots) or small traffic cones; 2
12- to 16-foot double-dutch ropes; "Jeopardy" game show music

DESCRIPTION

Arrange 12 rubber spots or traffic cones in a large circle (30–35-foot diameter) depicting a clock. Half the class represents the hour hand; the other half, the minute hand. Each team forms a single line and holds on to a long single rope. Teams start at 12:00 position.

When a time is called, e.g., 6:00, 4:30, 10:45, etc., teams align themselves in the appropriate positions. Use the music as a timing method for students to perform the correct positions.

MODIFICATION

• Make two separate teams and see which one can perform the correct response first.

ACTIVITY

Clue

CONCEPT

ACADEMIC
(Deduction)

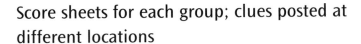

EQUIPMENT

Score sheets for each group; clues posted at
different locations

DESCRIPTION

Place sequential clues at six to eight different sites. By arranging
locations in a zigzag formation, the running distance increases
dramatically. Divide students into groups of four. Distribute clue
sheets and assign different starting points for each team. Once a clue
is found, team members write down the secret code and read the
next clue. Score sheets are collected to check for accuracy.

SAMPLE CLUES:

#	Clue	Secret Code (write down)
1.	*The game starts at home plate.*	*Seven*
2.	*Look for something you climb.*	*Days*
3.	*Enter here for fitness and fun.*	*Without*
4.	*The flag lives here.*	*Physical Education makes one weak.*

MODIFICATION

Use a math problem.

ACTIVITY

Whistler

CONCEPT

ACADEMIC (Sequencing)

EQUIPMENT

1 whistle

DESCRIPTION

"Whistler" is a thinking game that requires a rapid correct physical response to a designated signal. Like "Simon Says," students must perform the appropriate task with the associated number of whistle sounds. Incorrect responses result in a penalty. Each time there's a miscue, that student must touch all four walls before returning to the game. See how many of the cues your class can learn today.

The sequence is as follows:

1 blow	= jump up	6 blows	= jog in place
2 blows	= turn around	7 blows	= 1 push-up
3 blows	= sit down	8 blows	= 1 jumping jack
4 blows	= 1 bent-knee curl-up	9 blows	= balance on one foot
5 blows	= clap three times	10 blows	= lie on back

MODIFICATION

- Once all cues are learned, mix them up.
- Speed them up.

Road Warriors

CONCEPT

ACADEMIC (Traffic Signs)

EQUIPMENT

Road signs; traffic cones for marking off a figure-8 pattern; scooters for at least half the class

DESCRIPTION

Arrange students in partners and count off "1, 2." Even-numbered partners are drivers while odd-numbered students serve as traffic sign holders. They are spaced evenly around the infield and indicate to drivers what action to take. Holders of the yield signs situate themselves at the crossing between the middle of the figure-8.

Following a signal to begin, students sit and move backward through the pattern negotiating traffic signs as they go. After two to three minutes of pushing, drivers and sign holders switch places.

MODIFICATION

None.

ACTIVITY

Tic-Tac-Toe Basketball

CONCEPT

ACADEMIC (Sequencing)

EQUIPMENT

2–6 basketballs; chalk, tape, or carpeted grids; 4 separate colored beanbags per team

DESCRIPTION

Teams stand in single files 10 feet away from their goal. Balls are distributed to the first person in each line. Following a signal to begin, **one shot** is taken. If the basket is made, that player places his or her beanbag on the grid and gives the ball to the next person. If the basket is missed, that player returns the rebound to the next player in line and runs to the end of the line. The first team to place three of its beanbags in a tic-tac-toe line scores a point. When this occurs, beanbags are removed and a new game begins.

MODIFICATION

- Change the types of shots.
- Have students shoot from their choice of positions marked with vinyl polyspots.

30-Second Shap-Up

CONCEPT

ACADEMIC (Shapes)

EQUIPMENT

Shape cards: 20-foot piece of
elastic stretch rope (1/8-inch thick)

DESCRIPTION

Arrange students in a straight line
with both hands on a thin piece of
20- to 30-foot long elastic rope.
Once a shape card is shown by the
teacher, students have 30 seconds to
duplicate the picture shown.

MODIFICATION

- Have older students attempt to copy the shape of their state.
  Individuals can stand inside marking major cities, rivers, mountain
  ranges, etc.
- Students in one group can compete against a second for speed.

Part Three

Assessment

It is no longer acceptable to evaluate children entirely on a single standard or test. Portfolios paint a representative picture of the students' cognitive (knowledge), affective (values), and psychomotor (performance) progress.

Ready-to-Use Pre-Sport Skills Activities Program provides a variety of pathways from which students can be evaluated in *active* situations. The 100 theme-oriented lessons and game forms included here mirror the types of activities represented in the NASPE's national standards. The *Take Home* assignments and related monthly calendars extend the classroom experiences into the home.

The following are just a few authentic assessment samples that can make up a representative student portfolio.

P.E. REPORT CARD

September ___ Age ___

TEACHER _____

FITNESS SKILL MASTERS

REPORT PERIOD	MILE RUN Student runs or walks a mile as fast as possible. Score is measured in minutes & seconds. Score	ARM HANG or PULL-UPS With an overhand grip student holds chin over a bar (scored in seconds) . . . or pulls chin over a bar from a full extension (# of times). Score	CURL-UPS Student lies down with legs bent, and arms folded. Touch elbows to thighs as many times as possible in one minute. Score	SHUTTLE RUN Two beanbags are carried back & forth (1 at a time) between 2 lines 30 feet apart. Score in seconds. Score	V-REACH Sitting w/legs straight 12" apart, student reaches out as far as possible. A reach past the heels is scored in plus inches. Score	TOTAL POINTS

NAME

		P O I N T S	P O I N T S	P O I N T S	P O I N T S
1					
2					
3					

	Hand-stands	Juggling	Double-Unders	10 Sec. Speed
	T I M E	T O S S E S	J U M P S	N U M B E R

FREE MOUNT & RIDE

SCATS — TEAM MEMBER

PURPLE STAR

BLACK STAR

Handstands — 10 seconds / 1 minute
Juggling — 10 tosses / 100 tosses
Double-unders — 10 jumps / 100 jumps
10-Second Speed — 30 / 50

Cooperative Corner

NEEDS WORK

T = Needs more time to develop
NS = Not scored this reporting period

85 POINTS EARNS A T-SHIRT

28 points — BLUE STAR
19 points — ORANGE STAR
18 points — RED STAR
17 points — GREEN STAR

SPORT SKILLS

ACCURACY PITCH

FREE THROWS

SOCCER JUGGLING

10+ 9 8 7 6 5 4 3 2 1

Students are tested to see how many times in a row they can complete each skill. [Heights and distances may be modified to age-appropriate levels.]

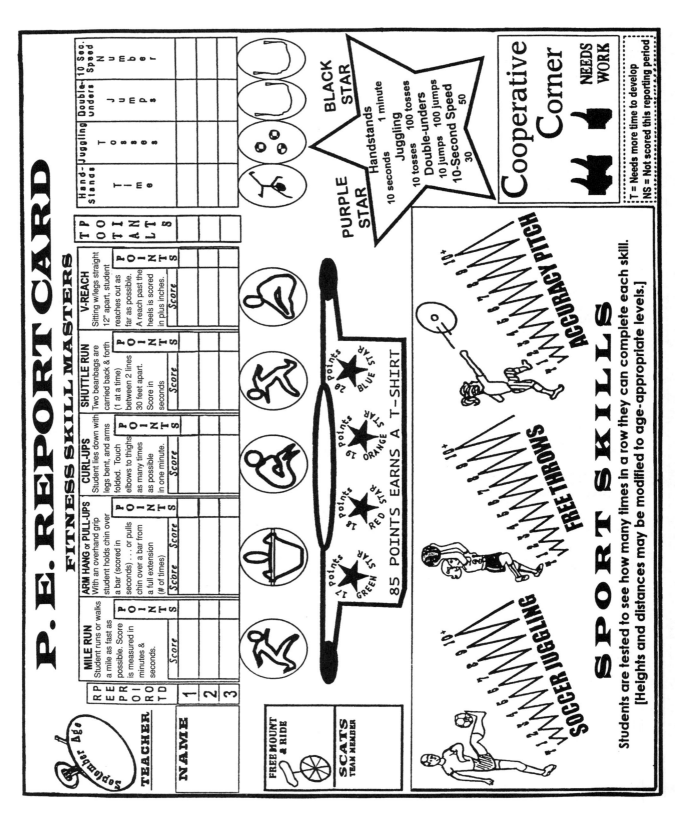

A.C.T.I.V.E.

A LESSON ASSESSMENT TOOL

A simple method for increasing the quality of a lesson is through the use of the A.C.T.I.V.E. acronym. Lesson designs that include these components do much to assure student success, motivation, and a desire to attempt new skills.

A = **All students active** (Historically, physical education has not done a good job at properly activating its customers. Skills do not improve while standing in a long line with one ball.)

C = **Creativity** (Creativity in the choice of equipment, game form, or manner of answering the task generates excitement and higher-level thinking skills.)

T = **Teaching Lifetime Fitness** (Concepts incorporating health-related fitness, nutrition, and lifestyle behaviors are integral to the development of all students regardless of their age.)

I = **Integration** (Including academic concepts in movement lessons can increase student understanding and build a stronger bond between the classroom and physical education staff.)

V = **Victimless Delivery Systems** (The old days of being picked last, one ball for 25 students, and only 50% of a class experiencing success is not in the best interest of our students or our professional image.)

E = **Equitable Experiences for All** (High expectations for all students regardless of gender, age, size, current level of ability, or interest is key to establishing a true *success-oriented* physical education program.)

NAME _____

GRADE _____

ROOM _____

During the next _____ weeks I will learn to _____

_____

_____

Teacher approval: _____ Date: _____

Progress week #1

_____

Progress week #2

_____

Progress week #3

_____

Accomplished: _____ Date: _____

Not Accomplished: _____

Comments: _____

_____

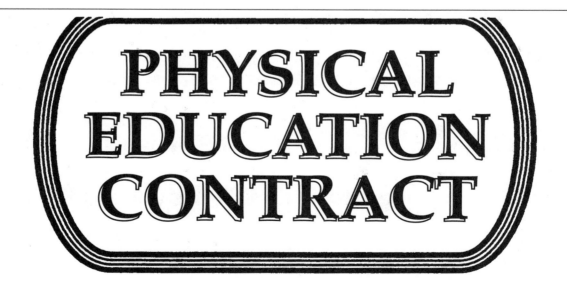

©2000 by Parker Publishing Company

SOCIAL I.Q.

Name: _____

Grade: _____

Room: _____

Rating

Criteria	Needs Improvement	Most Often	Always
• Follows directions			
• Self-directed			
• Cooperates with others			
• Sportsmanship			

Comments:

P.E. JOURNAL OF

BEST SCORES

Volleyball Passes

Handstands

Juggling

Double Unders

Speed Jumping

Shooting
(Consecutive shots made)

Soccer Juggling
(Consecutive hits)

Target Throwing
(Consecutive *"wall target"* hits)

Balance Beam Basics

Name: _____ Rm: _____

Can you ...  yes   no

- walk from one end to the other without falling off? _____ | _____
- perform the same task while moving backward? _____ | _____
- walk to the middle and make a full turn? _____ | _____
- walk to the middle and pick up a beanbag? _____ | _____
- walk to the middle and step through a partner-held hoop? _____ | _____
- balance a beanbag on your head and walk across? _____ | _____
- walk to the middle and touch one knee to the beam? _____ | _____
- bounce a ball on the floor while walking across? _____ | _____
- raise a foot above your head? _____ | _____
- perform a locomotor movement? _____ | _____

P.E. Teacher's Skill by Skill Activities Program
by Turner and Turner. Parker Publishing, 1989

SOFTBALL
SKILL ANALYSIS

Name: _____ **Rm:** _____

Teacher _____

(throwing)

	yes	no
• transfers weight with good form	___	___
• demonstrates accuracy	___	___
• follows through	___	___
• snaps wrist on release	___	___

(catching)

	yes	no
• moves to the ball	___	___
• hands in correct position (fingers up-balls high-down on balls low)	___	___
• uses two hands	___	___
• absorbs force on contact	___	___

*These skills were assessed by observing partners in facing lines 15–20 ft. apart and individually off walls.

Weekly P. E. Journal

Entry Date: _____

This week I learned how to: _____
_____
_____

I improved at: _____
_____
_____

Progress on my personal goals included: _____
_____
_____

This week I enjoyed working on: _____
_____
_____

My least favorite activity this week was: _____

Name: _____

Period: _____

Teacher: _____

Volleyball skill card of

○ **teacher's initials**

equipment:
balloons, vinyl or beach balls

teacher tips:
Join hands, interlock fingers, forearms provide flat surface, ball contact between wrist and elbows, arms away from body, knees bent, elbows locked on contact

Can you ...

- self pass and bump a ball 3 consecutive times? Five?
- bump your ball higher than your head 2 times in a row?
- bump, clap your hands, bump again? Clap twice?
- bump, touch the floor, and bump again?
- bump, make a full turn, and bump again?

when you have successfully completed these tasks, check with your teacher and move on to card 2

Success Stories

THIS WEEK IN P.E.

my most incredible feats were:

_____

_____

_____

_____

_____

Name: _____ Rm: _____

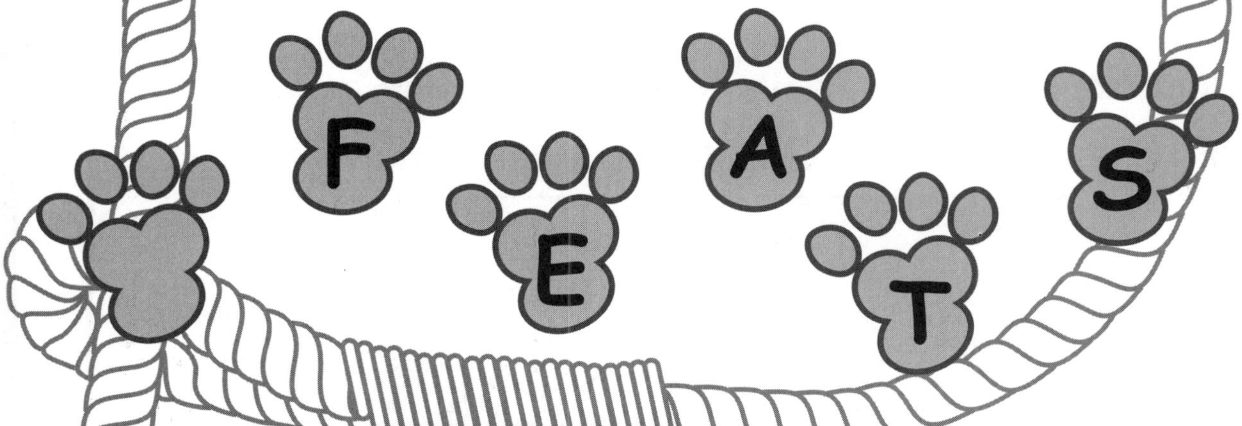

F E A T S

R R R

Recess Running Record
of

_____

Directions: Fill in one circle for each lap you complete.
Five laps = 1 mile.

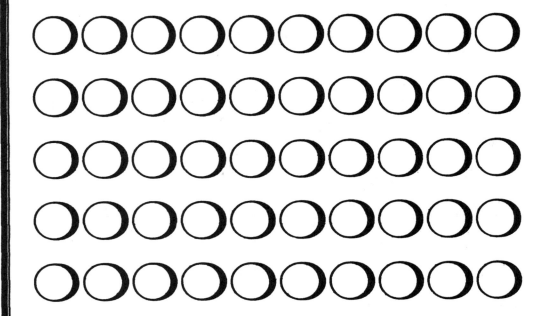

Congratulations! You have completed 10 miles.

Teacher: _____

STAMP IT OUT

Jump Rope Journal

for

_____

Directions: Practice each stunt. I will stamp each one you can do correctly.

SKIER

BELL

SIDE-
STRADDLE

SCISSORS

CHRIS CROSS

(_Illustrations:_ American Heart Association, _Curriculum Guide,_ 1991.)

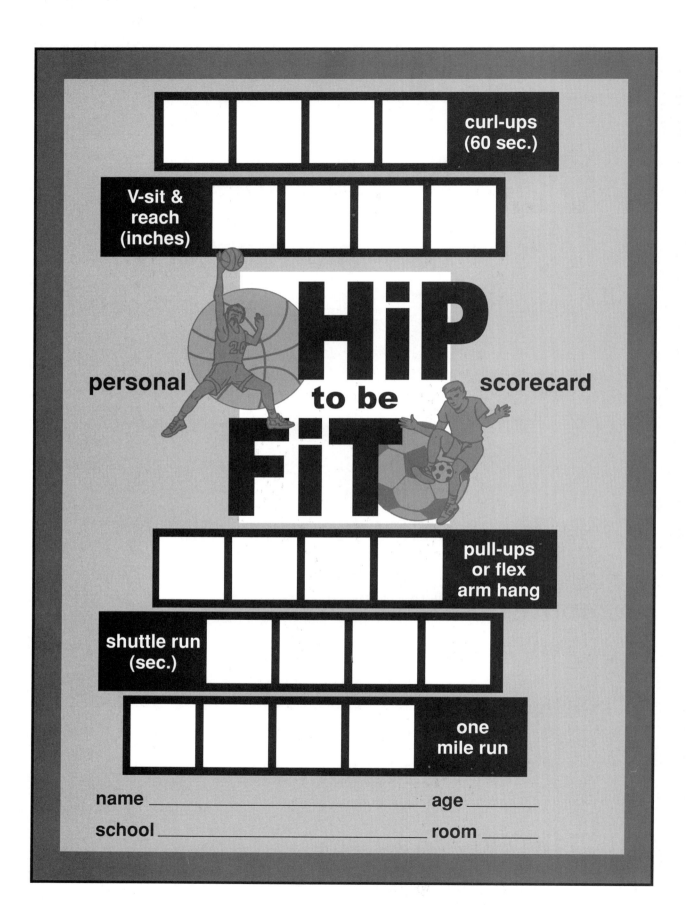

curl-ups
(60 sec.)

V-sit &
reach
(inches)

HiP
to be
FiT

personal   scorecard

pull-ups
or flex
arm hang

shuttle run
(sec.)

one
mile run

name _____ age _____

school _____ room _____

Part Four

ReiNForciNg The PoWer OF PHySicaL EducatioN

If a teacher doesn't believe a child can learn a certain skill, there's a good chance the child will feel the same way. If a curriculum is dominated by competitive activities, children will likely become more combative. If the teacher lacks energy and motivation, children will often mirror that adult standing in front of them.

Physical education, more than any other subject, has the potential to induce change. It can increase the self-confidence of an entire student body, raise the fitness level of a community, and alter misconceptions about the subject's ability to stimulate learning in other subjects as well.

The power of physical education is like electricity. The power can be turned on and turned off by one person—**the teacher.**

"All the well-meaning reform strategies in schools today—school uniforms, higher academic standards, tougher tests—can't supplant what research increasingly says is the single most important element in student success: a good teacher."

The Seattle Times, Sunday, November 9, 1998.

"We need to get the message out, loud and clear, that quality physical education for every child is a necessity—not a luxury."

Tom McMillen

PHYSICAL ACTIVITY

A Report from the Surgeon General of the United States

While the United States is looked upon as being a world leader in countless arenas, Americans are falling behind in the area of physical activity. In 1994, the Surgeon General of the United States published a document describing the importance of regular physical activity. Major conclusions from this report are listed below.

- People of all ages benefit from regular physical activity.
- With modest increases in daily activities, most Americans can improve their health and quality of life.
- Vigorous intensity produces greater results.
- Physical activity can reduce the risk of premature mortality in general, and of coronary heart disease, hypertension, colon cancer, and diabetes mellitus in particular. Physical activity also improves mental health and is important for the health of muscles, bones, and joints.
- More than 60 percent of American adults are not physically active on a regular basis. In fact, 25 percent of all adults are not active at all.
- Nearly half of American youth (ages 12–21) are not vigorously active on a regular basis.
- Daily enrollment in physical education classes has declined among high school students from 42 percent in 1991 to 25 percent in 1995.

Entertained, I sit
watching videos on my TV set.
Curled up in a big soft chair
surfing the Internet
without a care.
Exercise is too much trouble.
I feel like ice cream, maybe a double.

Bud Turner

Prevent Couch Potatoes

While They Are Still Small Fries!

Planned, Purposeful, Physical Education

NOTHING BEATS SUCCESS

A research study* conducted in 1995 described the experiences of low-skilled students in physical education. When analyzed, "all students liked physical education when they were successful."

Students are our customers
not our employees.
The experiences we offer
shape their destiny.

As adults, we tend to frequent businesses that provide the best services. Customer satisfaction keeps us coming back. When one child fails, the entire system is affected. Not only does the student's motivation to participate diminish, but the support for the profession as a whole is also jeopardized.

With 13 years' experience
I know how to stand in line,
suit up, follow your signals,
sand bag my times.

Now I am a graduate,
no more push-ups for me.
I am running for the school board.
Guess what my vote will be?

Bud Turner

*P.A. Portman, *"Who is having fun in physical education?" Journal of Teaching in Physical Education,* **1995, 14, 445–453.**

A QUALITY PROGRAM INCLUDES:

P = Planned, purposeful lesson designs

H = High expectations for all

Y = Youth-oriented curriculums

S = Safe learning environments

I = Individual successes every day

C = Caring adults

A = Academic concepts through movement

L = Leadership opportunities

EDUCATION

HIGH EXPECTATIONS = HIGH RESULTS

Primary students can accomplish incredibly complex skills. The only thing holding them back is **YOU.**

Physical Education Proclamation

"WE THE P.E. SPECIALISTS of this school district <u>commit</u> to the appropriate standards of action endorsed by our state and national professional organizations with regard to establishing quality, planned, purposeful, **SUCCESS-ORIENTED** physical education for <u>ALL</u> students regardless of their age, gender, ability, or current level of interest."

This pledge will assist in achieving the ultimate goal of physical education—to improve students' motor, cognitive, and affective development leading to a lifetime of healthy movement experiences.

Powerful P.E. Programs Possess:

- **<u>A CARING TEACHER</u>** with high expectations for all students.
- **<u>A CHILD-CENTERED, AGE-APPROPRIATE CURRICULUM</u>** that increases student's physical, social, and cognitive skills.
- **<u>A SAFE, POSITIVE LEARNING ENVIRONMENT</u>** promoting positive partnerships with parents and community.
- **<u>MULTIPLE OPPORTUNITIES FOR SUCCESS.</u>**

Management Strategies

USE:

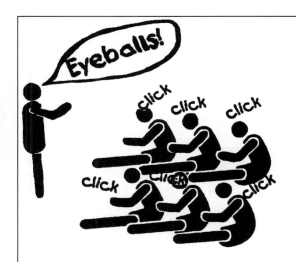

Start and stop signals that are consistent.

One piece of equipment for every child.

Small groups rather than large ones.

Modified rules that increase activity and opportunities for success.

Part Five

The New National Standards for Physical Education

The **National Standards for Physical Education** document is a product of several years of work by leading professionals. It indicates what children should know and be able to do at specific grade levels. The benchmarks provide teachers with excellent examples of assessments of movement proficiencies. The standards solidify physical education's place in the academic arena.

National Physical Education Standards for Kindergarten and Grade 2

Kindergarten

1. Demonstrates competency in many movement forms and proficiency in a few movement forms.
   <u>Sample Benchmarks</u>:
   a. Travels in forward and sideways directions using a variety of locomotor (nonlocomotor) patterns and changes direction quickly in response to a signal.
   b. Demonstrates clear contrasts between slow and fast movement while traveling.
   c. Walks and runs using mature form.
   d. Rolls sideways without hesitating or stopping.
   e. Tosses a ball and catches it before it bounces twice.
   f. Kicks a stationary ball using a smooth continuous running step.
   g. Maintains momentary stillness bearing weight on a variety of body parts.

2. Applies movement concepts and principles to the learning and development of motor skills.
   <u>Sample Benchmarks</u>:
   a. Walks, runs, hops, and skips in forward and sideways directions, and changes direction quickly in response to a signal.
   b. Identifies and uses a variety of relationships with objects (e.g., over/under, behind, alongside, through).
   c. Identifies and begins to utilize the technique employed (leg flexion) to soften the landing in jumping.

3. Exhibits a physically active lifestyle.
   <u>Sample Benchmarks</u>:
   a. Participates regularly in vigorous physical activity.
   b. Recognizes that physical activity is good for personal well-being.
   c. Identifies feelings that result from participation in physical activities.

4. Achieves and maintains a health-enhancing level of physical fitness.
   <u>Sample Benchmarks</u>:
   a. Sustains moderate to vigorous physical activity.
   b. Is aware of his or her heart beating fast during physical activity.

5. Demonstrates responsible personal and social behavior in physical activity settings.
   <u>Sample Benchmarks</u>:
   a. Knows the rules for participating in the gymnasium and on the playground.
   b. Works in a group setting without interfering with others.
   c. Responds to teacher signals for attention.
   d. Responds to rule infractions when reminded once.
   e. Follows directions given to the class for an all-class activity.
   f. Handles equipment safety by putting it away when not in use.
   g. Takes turns using a piece of equipment.
   h. Transfers rules of the gym to "rules of the playground."

6. Demonstrates understanding and respect for differences among people in physical activity settings.
   <u>Sample Benchmarks</u>:
   a. Enjoys participation alone and with others.
   b. Chooses playmates without regard to personal differences (e.g., race, gender, disability).

7. Understands that physical activity provides the opportunity for enjoyment, challenge, self expression, and social interaction.
   <u>Sample Benchmarks</u>:
   a. Enjoys participation alone and with others.
   b. Identifies feelings that result from participation in physical activities.
   c. Looks forward to physical education classes.

Credit: *Moving into the Future, National Physical Education Standards: A Guide to Content and Assessment.* Developed by the National Association for Sport and Physical Education, WCB McGraw Hill, 1995.

Grade 2

1. Demonstrates competency in many movement forms and proficiency in a few movement forms.
   <u>Sample Benchmarks</u>:
   a. Demonstrates skills of chasing, fleeing, and dodging to avoid others.
   b. Combines locomotor patterns in time to music.
   c. Balances, demonstrating momentary stillness, in symmetrical and nonsymmetrical shapes on a variety of body parts.
   d. Receives and sends an object in a continuous motion.
   e. Strikes a ball repeatedly with a paddle.

2. Applies movement concepts and principles to the learning and development of motor skills.
   <u>Sample Benchmarks</u>:
   a. Identifies four characteristics of a mature throw.
   b. Uses concepts of space awareness and movement control to run, hop, and skip in different ways in a large group without bumping into others or falling.

c. Identifies and demonstrates the major characteristics of mature walking, running, hopping, and skipping.

3. Exhibits a physically active lifestyle.
   <u>Sample Benchmarks</u>:
   a. Seeks participation in gross motor activity of a moderate to vigorous nature.
   b. Participates in a wide variety of activities that involve locomotion, nonlocomotion, and manipulation of objects outside of physical education class.
   c. Willingly completes physical education activity "homework" assignments.

4. Achieves and maintains a health-enhancing level of physical fitness.
   <u>Sample Benchmarks</u>:
   a. Sustains activity for longer periods of time while participating in chasing or fleeing, traveling activities in physical education, and/or on the playground.
   b. Identifies changes in the body during vigorous physical activity.
   c. Supports body weight for climbing, hanging, and momentarily taking weight on hands.
   d. Moves each joint through a full range of motion.

5. Demonstrates responsible personal and social behavior in physical activity settings.
   <u>Sample Benchmarks</u>:
   a. Uses equipment and space safely and properly.
   b. Responds positively to an occasional reminder about a rule infraction.
   c. Practices specific skills as assigned until the teacher signals the end of practice.
   d. Stops activity immediately at the signal to do so.
   e. Honestly reports the results of work.
   f. Invites a peer to take his or her turn at a piece of apparatus before repeating a turn.
   g. Assists partner by sharing observations about skill performance during practice.

6. Demonstrates understanding and respect for differences among people in physical activity settings.
   <u>Sample Benchmarks</u>:
   a. Appreciates the benefits that accompany cooperation and sharing.
   b. Displays consideration of others in physical activity settings.
   c. Demonstrates the elements of socially acceptable conflict resolution.

7. Understands that physical activity provides the opportunity for enjoyment, challenge, self-expression, and social interaction.
   <u>Sample Benchmarks</u>:
   a. Appreciates the benefits that accompany cooperation and sharing.
   b. Accepts the feelings resulting from challenges, successes, and failures in physical activity.
   c. Willingly tries new activities.

National Physical Education Standards for Grades 4 and 6

Grade 4

1. Demonstrates competency in many movement forms and proficiency in a few movement forms.
   <u>Sample Benchmarks</u>:
   a. Throws, catches, and kicks using mature form.
   b. Dribbles and passes a basketball to a moving receiver.
   c. Balances with control on a variety of objects (balance board, large apparatus, skates).
   d. Develops and refines a gymnastics sequence demonstrating smooth transitions.
   e. Develops and refines a creative dance sequence into a repeatable pattern.
   f. Jumps and lands for height/distance using mature form.

2. Applies movement concepts and principles to the learning and development of motor skills.
   <u>Sample Benchmarks</u>:
   a. Transfers weight from feet to hands at fast and slow speeds using large extensions (e.g., mule kick, handstand, cartwheel).
   b. Accurately recognizes the critical elements of a throw made by a fellow student and provides feedback to that student.
   c. Consistently strikes a softly thrown ball with a bat or paddle demonstrating an appropriate grip.
   d. Understands that appropriate practice improves performance.

3. Exhibits a physically active lifestyle.
   <u>Sample Benchmarks</u>:
   a. Regularly participates in physical activity for the purpose of developing a healthy lifestyle.
   b. Describes healthful benefits that result from regular and appropriate participation in physical activity.
   c. Identifies at least one activity that they participate in on a regular basis (formal or informal).
   d. Is beginning to be aware of opportunities for more formal participation in physical activities in the community.

4. Achieves and maintains a health-enhancing level of physical fitness.
   <u>Sample Benchmarks</u>:
   a. Engages in appropriate activity that results in the development of muscular strength.
   b. Maintains continuous aerobic activity for a specified time and/or activity.
   c. Supports, lifts, and controls body weight in a variety of activities.
   d. Regularly participates in physical activity for the purpose of improving physical fitness.

5. Demonstrates responsible personal and social behavior in physical activity settings.
   Sample Benchmarks:
   a. When given the opportunity, arranges gymnastics equipment safely in a manner appropriate to the task.
   b. Takes seriously their role to teach an activity or skill to two other classmates.
   c. Works productively with a partner to improve the overhand throw pattern for distance by using the critical elements of the process.
   d. Accepts the teacher's decision regarding a personal rule infraction without displaying negative reactions toward others.
   e. Assesses their own performance problems without blaming others.

6. Demonstrates understanding and respect for differences among people in physical activity settings.
   Sample Benchmarks:
   a. Recognizes differences and similarities in others' physical activity.
   b. Indicates respect for persons from different backgrounds and the cultural significance they attribute to various games, dances, and physical activities.
   c. Demonstrates acceptance of the skills and abilities of others through verbal and nonverbal behavior.

7. Understands that physical activity provides the opportunity for enjoyment, challenge, self-expression, and social interaction.
   Sample Benchmarks:
   a. Experience positive feelings as a result of involvement in physical activity.
   b. Design games, gymnastics, and dance sequences that are personally interesting.
   c. Celebrate personal successes and achievements as well as those of others.

Grade 6

1. Demonstrates competency in many movement forms and proficiency in a few movement forms.
   a. Throws a variety of objects demonstrating both accuracy and force (e.g., basketball, footballs, frisbees).
   b. Hand dribbles and foot dribbles while preventing an opponent from stealing the ball.
   c. Designs and performs gymnastics and dance sequences that combine traveling, rolling, balancing, and weight transfer into smooth flowing sequences with intentional changes in direction, speed, flow.
   d. Keeps an object going continuously with a partner using a striking pattern.
   e. Places the ball away from an opponent in a racket sport activity.

2. Applies movement concepts and principles to the learning and development of motor skills.
   a. Detects, analyzes and corrects errors in personal movement patterns.
   b. Identifies proper warm-up and cool-down techniques and the reasons for using them.
   c. Identifies basic practice and conditioning principles that enhance performance.

3. Exhibits a physically active lifestyle.
   a. Chooses to exercise at home for personal enjoyment and benefit.
   b. Participates in games, sports, dance and outdoor pursuits both in and out of school based on individual interests and capabilities.
   c. Identifies opportunities close to home for participation in different kinds of activities.

4. Achieves and maintains a health-enhancing level of physical fitness.
   a. Keeps a record of heart rate before, during and after vigorous physical activity.
   b. Participates in fitness-enhancing organized physical activities outside of school (e.g., gymnastic clubs, community sponsored youth sports).
   c. Engages in physical activity at the target heart rate for a minimum of 20 minutes.
   d. Correctly demonstrates activities designed to improve and maintain muscular strength and endurance, flexibility, cardiorespiratory functioning, and proper body composition.

5. Demonstrates responsible personal and social behavior in physical activity settings.
   Sample Benchmarks:
   a. Makes responsible decisions about using time, applying rules, and following through with the decisions made.
   b. Uses time wisely when given the opportunity to practice and improve performance.
   c. Makes suggestions for modifications in a game or activity that can improve the game.
   d. Remains on-task in a group activity without close teacher monitoring.
   e. Chooses a partner that he or she can work with productively.
   f. Distinguishes between acts of "courage" and reckless acts.
   g. Includes concerns for safety in self-designed activities.

6. Demonstrates understanding and respect for differences among people in physical activity settings.
   Sample Benchmarks:
   a. Recognizes the role of games, sports, and dance in getting to know and understand others of like and different backgrounds.
   b. Through verbal and nonverbal behavior demonstrates cooperation with peers of different gender, race, ethnicity in a physical activity setting.
   c. Seek out, participate with, and show respect for persons of like and different skill levels.
   d. Recognizes the importance of one's personal heritage.

7. Understands that physical activity provides the opportunity for enjoyment, challenge, self-expression, and social interaction.
   Sample Benchmarks:
   a. Recognizes the role of games, sports, and dance in getting to know and understand self and others.
   b. Identifies benefits resulting from participation in different forms of physical activities.
   c. Describes ways to use the body and movement activities to communicate ideas and feelings.
   d. Seeks physical activity in informal settings that utilize skills and knowledge gained in physical education classes.